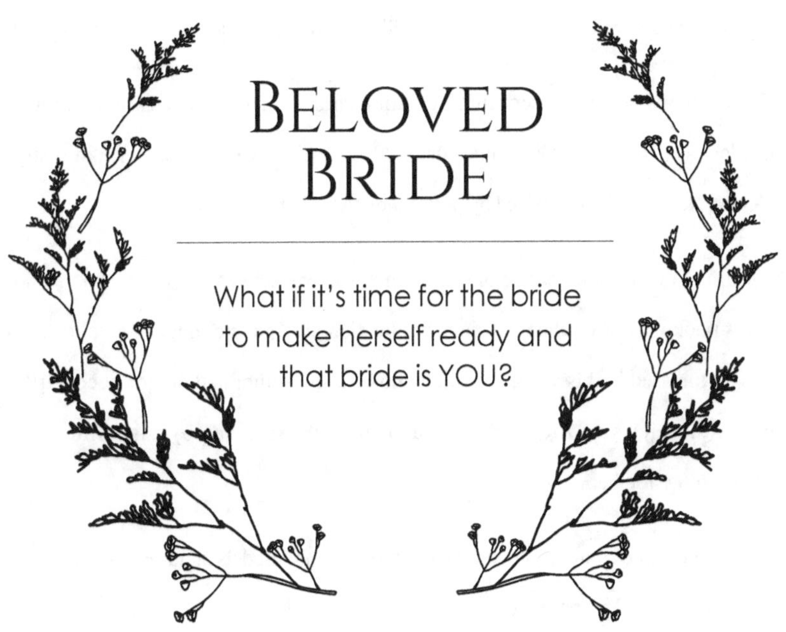

BELOVED BRIDE

What if it's time for the bride
to make herself ready and
that bride is YOU?

RHONDA DE LA MORINIERE

Library of Congress Control Number:

Print information available on last page.

ISBN- 979-8-9874084-9-0

TO MATTHEW DE LA MORINIERE,

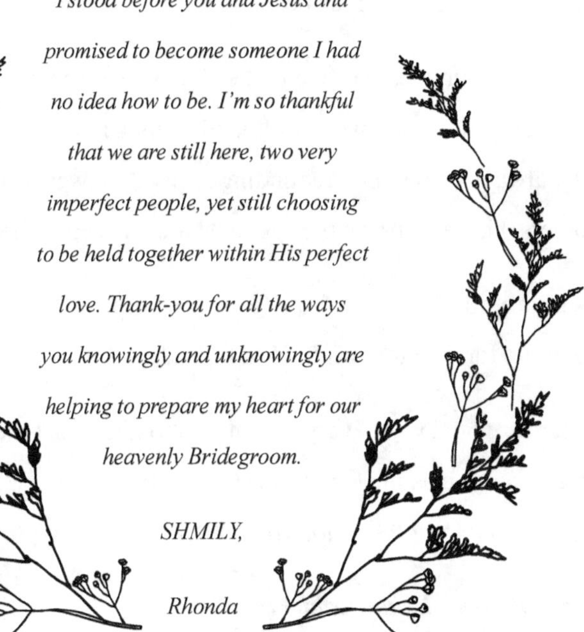

I stood before you and Jesus and

promised to become someone I had

no idea how to be. I'm so thankful

that we are still here, two very

imperfect people, yet still choosing

to be held together within His perfect

love. Thank-you for all the ways

you knowingly and unknowingly are

helping to prepare my heart for our

heavenly Bridegroom.

SHMILY,

Rhonda

I would like to take an opportunity to acknowledge someone who has been used by God to help me get this book birthed into the world.

Without Brenda Berlingeri, I am not so sure this book would be here today. As a long time member of my first group of Bible study ladies, she fell in love with this study and was the first to insist that I change the name from *One Bride to Beloved Bride.* In her words, "we are His Beloved!"

Her calls, texts, and instant messages always arrived just in time, always asking the same question "have you published the book, yet?"

Brenda, your questions were like Christ's whispers to my heart (okay, let's be real, sometimes more like His megaphone). Sometimes loud, yet always convicting, reminding me that, however unknown I am to others, I have a known purpose to share all He has shown me.

I love you and thank-you for your help in encouraging me and praying for me until this book was ready.

Brenda would want every one of you to know that these words are as real over you as they are to her, *"I am my beloved's, and my beloved is mine; he feedeth his flock among the lilies."(Song of Soloman 6:3)*

Your Beloved Bride Sister Forever,

Rhonda

I also want to acknowledge all my sisters who have faithfully walked beside me as we've journeyed with Him. You have no idea who often your faces, your words, and the many memories of our time together have touched my heart and brought me encouragement to remember Who I'm doing this for and how important it is. I thank you each for being my bridesmaids and allowing me the beautiful privilege of getting to peep at you behind your wedding veils. You are truly the MOST BEAUTIFUL brides of all! *"You yourselves are our letter of recommendation, written on our hearts, to be known and read by all." (2 Corinthians 3:2).*

And lastly, I want to acknowledge you, wherever you are, whoever you are, for taking the time to let Jesus, our Beloved Bridegroom, take you by the hand to lead you to the place you most belong, His heart. May you truly encounter His love and His identity over you as His Beloved Bride.

Table of Contents

Introduction

"And I will betroth you to me forever. I will betroth you to me in righteousness and in justice, in steadfast love and in mercy. I will betroth you to me in faithfulness. And you shall know the LORD."

(Hosea 2:19-20)

We are about to walk through a life changing journey together, one that will change the way you see yourself, purpose, and the world around you. Before you were born, Jesus looked upon you and whispered these words over you, "you shall know the Lord." Against the dark backdrop of this world, He's laid out a scarlet trail, the wedding aisle of His love for you, upon which He invites you to rise and shine and know that He is both your Lord and Bridegroom.

We will discover how this marriage took place as we walk through each step of an ancient Hebrew wedding. We will not only witness how Jesus fulfilled each one, but also take time to absorb these moments, making them personal to each of our individual lives. You will discover your own love story with the Savior as you see Him through the rightful lens of your beloved Bridegroom, who has and is already carrying the weight of your life across the threshold of this earthly experience. You will discover Him to be the most faithful Bridegroom.

This study has changed my life more than any other has. It has changed the way I see eternity, which has changed the way I see my marriage, my mothering, and each moment of my existence. I know it will do the same for you as you discover your identity and begin to live as the bride of Christ. At one time in my life, my experiences in this world seemed so big and real, even bigger, and more real than Jesus. Yet, as He began to reveal Himself to me through the lens of the Bridegroom, He became the substance I lived in, eclipsing every other earthly experience in His shadow.

We live in a world where a covenant or promise means very little. So much so, that it may harden our hearts towards believing that even God can keep His promise to us. Yet, as we look to Jesus, and see that He not only kept His covenant promise to us but is keeping it still. In Him, we have a sure place to stand beneath our feet, and as we contemplate our role as His bride, we will find ourselves standing in this place too.

Too often, we trust Jesus for salvation and then begin to journey along a weighty path of following our own expectations of who we are in Him. After all, we made a promise and now we must keep it, right?

We confuse trusting our promises to Jesus with trusting His promise to us. Until, after countless tries to follow Him, we began to sink under the weight of it all and either start pretending, performing, or walk away completely.

As we will discover through this journey together, being His bride has never been about what we do, it's always been about who we have become because of all He's done.

As He expresses in Hosea 2:19-20, "And I will betroth you to me forever. I will betroth you to me in righteousness and in justice, in steadfast love and in mercy. I will betroth you to me in faithfulness. And you shall know the LORD."

The weight of our journey has already fallen upon His shoulders, and we get to spend our lives allowing Him to carry us through the beauty and wonder of who we truly become once we became His.

We will begin with a wedding itinerary, which will include Hebrew terms that are important for our study.

Each week's study will begin with taking one more step down our ancient Hebrew wedding aisle, as we examine both the ancient Hebrew cultural portion of the ceremony as well as how Jesus fulfilled it and is fulfilling it in our lives.

There will be a weekly study available, that can help make these moments more personal to your own life as you allow your heart to interact with what you are learning about Jesus' marriage to you. I strongly encourage you to read the weekly Bible study along with this book as they are intended to go together to help you fully enter your experience as the bride of Christ. Remember, this journey is about understanding who you've become as Christ's bride. The study portion allow you that opportunity.

I encourage you to take your time and enjoy your walk down the wedding aisle with Jesus. Give yourself time to see the beauty of who you've become through His grace. Revelation 19:7 says, *"Let us exalt and give him glory, for the marriage of the Lamb has come, and His Bride has made herself ready."* There comes a time for every bride when she must look in the mirror as she is and prepare herself for who she's becoming as His bride.

This is your moment.

Welcome, beloved bride.

TERMS AND DEFINITIONS

B'rit: Covenant (sealed in blood), Old Testament.

B'rit Hadashah: New Covenant, Tanakh, sealed in Christ's blood.

Kidushin: This is the betrothal period (think of Mary and Joseph), this is the name given for the period after the first part of the wedding takes place, in preparation for the second part. It usually lasts anywhere from one to two years; however, no one knows when the second part will begin except the groom's father. The father watches over the son as he builds the dwelling place for his bride and the father determines when that dwelling is ready and complete as he announces to his son, "Go get your bride," once his desired completion for the dwelling is finished by his son.

Ketubah: This refers to the wedding contract. It is presented to the bride on her wedding day and signed at the second part of the wedding by the bride. It is the bridegroom's covenant to his bride, displaying all the promise he intends to her as well as his assuming full responsibility for her body, soul, and spirit. All of who she is will be transferred upon his shoulders should she accept his covenant promise to her. Our Ketubah is God's Word, His New Covenant to us as written in the New Testament. It's important to note that the bride has no part in this contract save that of receiving it, should she decide to enter it. The full weight of these promises rest upon the bridegroom's shoulders.

Mohar: Bride price. This is what it cost the bridegroom's father to purchase the bride. It is indicative of the value the father and son saw in the bride. Our Mohar is the blood of Christ, the Father's Son.

Kallah: Bride or "set apart one." Once sealed during the first portion of the wedding ceremony, the bride wears a veil over her face in public, as a demonstration that she has been "set apart" for betrothal. We are "set apart" in Christ, sealed through His Holy Spirit through Whom we demonstrate to the world that we are taken and betrothed to Christ, sealed for His glory.

Mikvah: Hebrew for baptism (more precisely, immersion). This is the bride's time for beautification. Jewish family tradition states that a woman is to re-do this each month after her cycle, as she becomes "new" again for her husband. The bride is to be fully submerged in a living body of water, symbolizing her new birth. Her first Mikvah takes place before the second portion of the wedding begins. Our Mikvah is our baptism as we are washed away from our old life, cleansed and made new in Christ. He also washes us in His Word throughout our journey with Him. He is our Living Water as we walk beside Him as His bride.

Chadar (Kadar): This is the wedding chamber. It is presented in the second portion of the wedding. It is the bride's house that the bridegroom has added on to his father's house. It is what he was building while his wife was in her time of preparation and waiting. Jesus is working on this right now as He is building His church (bride), while at the same time in heaven building a literal place for us to dwell eternally with Him.

Aperion: The bridal litter. This was a special carriage that was prepared for the bride, carried on the backs of the groomsmen, it transported the bride to her awaiting bridegroom at the call of the groom's father to begin the second portion of the wedding. She literally meets her groom in the air. For us, this gives reference to the Rapture of Christ's church, His bride.

The Huppah: The original meaning is room or covering. It is where the bride and groom will enter to consummate their marriage and where they will stay for seven days as they "yada" (get to know one another intimately) for the first time. Perhaps this is where we will spend seven years with our Bridegroom/ King just after the rapture as we finally get to know Him face to face.

CHAPTER ONE

THE FIRST HALF OF THE WEDDING

Imagine you are a young woman from Galilee over two-thousand years ago. Your father is a fisherman and you, your sister, and your mom help earn extra income by drying herbs to mix with grain to bake the best bread in town. The scent of fresh baking bread in the clay brick oven, mixed with the salty smell of the sea upon your father's robe fill the air. The sound of prayers echo through the small, two room home before dinner, a sacred reminder that you are God's people, and every detail of your life is lived in remembrance of this sacred call. You are fifteen and your changing body invites a mixture of both fear and wonder. Fear because the changes present opportunity for marriage and motherhood, two roles that in your culture represent God's most sacred and weighty calling. *"Taken out of man, and the two shall become one."*

At night, you lie on the soft cot beneath you and listen to the breathing of those around you, each one a gift given by God, yet carried about through His sacred cooperation with man. What will life be like when you are the one called upon to cooperate with God to take part in His holy plan for His people?

Just an ordinary girl, yet also part of God's most sacred call. *"I will make you a great nation, and I will bless you and make your name great, so you will be a blessing,"* (Genesis 12:2). This ordinary life seems a vast contrast to the holy and divine mystery that lies in your heritage. You gulp in remembrance of Who spoke the above words, at the very beginning, He called through Father Abraham.

You exist today, a living testimony that God's words are greater than any attempt to extinguish you. Glimpses of light streak through the room, piercing down the small slivers in your thatch roof, *"Look toward the heaven, and number the stars, if you are able to number them, so shall your offspring be." (Genesis 15:5).*

Stars bringing forth stars!

You wonder if God might perhaps be glimpsing down at you, lying there. Perhaps He sees slivers of light too, in the form of His people, breaking through earth's dark backdrop, bursting forth remembrance of His promise. Somehow God chose you to belong to Him, to be His camp on earth. Such a small life yet carrying the weight of such a big promise. Caught up in the wonder of it all, you drift off to sleep.

The next day, there is a knock at your door. Your heart races with a mixture of both dread and excitement as you hear men's voices echo from the next room. You recognize that tone in your father's voice, a solemn voice, usually reserved for moments of great emotion. Heart pounds and cheeks flush as you hear your name spoken through these unfamiliar voices.

Panic floods through your now shaking body as the thought jolts you, "could this be my wedding day?"

Both tenderness and fear burst through your heart as you hear your father call, "Leah, come," at once you suddenly become aware that this is it, the day God has planned for you before you were ever born, your wedding day!

Needing comfort, you set your eyes to your father's whose own eyes seem to have taken on an expression you've never noticed before. He is looking at you in a way he never has, as if you are a lamb being prepared for sacrifice.

It's all too much for you as you turn your eyes to the floor, hoping to find solace in something familiar. Dirt, how can such a sacred moment take place on such ordinary floors? Dirt and water, wasn't that how God made man? Nothing more than dirt and water, until He breathed life into him.

These were the thoughts that filled your mind as you let your eyes wander to him. Something about seeing his feet tendered your heart and brought you comfort. He is man, both vulnerable and afraid, yet he is standing here ready to choose you to become part of God's most holy plan, that of extending his family.

The sound of wine poured into a cup sobers you as you realize that soon the cup will be passed to you, and should you drink, you will have a whole new identity. Although you will still be in this home, nothing about your life or purpose will be the same.

As the Ketubah is read, your heart can only think of one thing, "how will you know?" Will God's voice burst through your heart, just as He did to Samuel as he laid on his bed in the temple? You've always envisioned that God might somehow prepare you in some sacred way for when this moment would come. Yet, it's here on this ordinary day, and you, just an ordinary girl, are being called to become part of His extraordinary plan.

You fear what will happen when your eyes meet his. What if you do not know? How will you respond? Will you disappoint both God and your father?

The Ketubah has been read, and you hear your father taking the drink, and you know the moment of decision is upon you, and all before you've even set eyes on the man who will become your husband, should you choose to take the drink.

Without even thinking you glance up into his face and know at once you are caught. Giggles burst out from you without even thinking as the sheer oddity of this moment hit's you like the weight of a king's stallion. Such an irreverent response to such a reverent moment, yet you can sense in his eyes the relief that comes at seeing your smile. You know at once that you will always remember this moment, the moment your eyes met for the first time.

The cup is in your hand now and you know that you have suddenly crossed a threshold you can never uncross. "Fill my cup with wine," the words come out through your lips, only a child a moment ago, yet now you stand as a bride, a woman who has taken her place in God's sacred destiny.

His eyes are locked on yours as you take the sip, sealing your future, entrusting it to him. Feelings you've never experienced before flood through your body. And even though your vows would not be consummated for at least a year or two, you both seemed to be locked into a moment of intimacy that you wished would never end.

He comes closer to you now, his eyes almost drinking in every part of you, as his spoken words over you flood your heart, "I consecrate you to me." His hands brush your cheek as he places the veil over your face and the gold coin around your forehead.

In one moment, you have changed in every way.

Before you even understood what was happening, you became someone completely new.

Near panic stirs your heart as you realize this wedding that you had no idea was coming, is now nearly over, at least the first part.

As you hear his voice speaking over you, you try to absorb every ounce of him with your whole heart. For you know that in but a moment he will be gone, leaving only a longing in your heart for the next phase of your wedding to take place.

His eyes seem to be drinking you into himself, as his voice speaks tenderly over you, "And if I go and prepare a place for you, I will come back and take you to be with me that you also may be where I am."

And as he and his father turn to make their way home, you know he has taken your heart with him. You would never be the same again for you have become his beloved bride.

The Cup, the Kallah, and the Coin

The first question God asked in the Bible can be found in Genesis 3:9, *"Where are you?"* It was just after the Fall when Adam and his wife were hiding from God. It represented the birth of mans' separation from his Creator.

We each begin our journey from a place of temporary dwelling, yet our hearts long for our eternal home.

And we find our way home as we let ourselves belong to Christ, our beloved Bridegroom. As we often discover, both as brides here on earth, as well as the bride of Christ, we often have no idea how to truly be who we have become.

Yet, as we will discover along this journey, our role has more to do with being as opposed to doing and believing as opposed to knowing.

So, sit back and enjoy this walk down the wedding aisle as you discover, by Christ's grace, who you've become as His bride.

This week, we will take time to truly examine our camp, where Jesus is headed to meet us, and to ask us to become His. We will spend this week using an Old Testament encounter to confront ourselves with the truth of our answer to Jesus as He asks us, "will you belong to Me, will you be My bride?"

A Hebrew wedding is divided into two parts, and the two are often separated by a long period of time, anywhere from one to two years. Today, we will go over the first part of the wedding, in Hebrew called the Erusin which means sanctification. It includes the Kiddushin, which means; holy, set apart, or veiled.

The Erusin begins when the father of the groom, and his son go to the bride's house with a cup and a skin of wine to make his intentions known. As the young man goes to the house of the girl, he initially must carry four things. The first is the Mohar, or bride price, which is a large sum of money (or many expensive items) paid to the father of the bride for the cost of his daughter. Next is the Matan, which was a gift given from the bridegroom to his bride. It served as an insurance that he would be back for her since there would be a long time between the first portion of the wedding and second. It also served as a reminder to her of her new identity as his. It was often a gold coin (or coins), which she would wear upon her forehead as a sign to the world that she was a Kallah, a set apart one, a complete one, a bride. The Ketubah was next, it was the betrothal contract that included all the promises the bridegroom was making to his bride. Lastly, the wedding cup was to be brought along as well as a skin of wine, as it was necessary to seal the marriage covenant through drinking the wine.

As the father of the groom and his son enter the bride's home, the father of the groom would open the wineskin, pour it into the cup and drink, and then pass it to his son, who would drink and offer it to the father of the bride, who, after drinking would present the cup to his daughter who would be invited to the table to hear the Ketubah (bridal contract). Should she agree to the bridegroom's promises presented to her, she would turn her cup over and say, "fill my cup." And once she drank, she was considered married from that moment on.

As we read this, we must ask ourselves some questions to help us understand our own place in this wedding process.

First, did Jesus come to our house?

John 1:9 answers this for us, *"The true light, which enlightens everyone was coming into the world."* Another scripture that answers our question is John 1:14 in the amplified version, *"The Word (Christ) became flesh, and lived among us; and we (actually) saw His glory, glory as belongs to the (One and) only begotten Son of the Father, (the only Son who is truly unique, the One of His kind, who is) full of grace and truth (absolutely free of deception.)*

Secondly, did He come with His Father?

One place in scripture that assures us that He did is found in John 14:8-9 where Jesus and Phillip have an exchange that clearly answers our question, *"Phillip said to him, Lord, show us the Father, and it is enough for us, Jesus said to Him, Have I been with you so long, and still you do not know me, Phillip? Whoever has seen me has seen the Father."*

Jesus was God, yet because He was also becoming our Way, He walked in perfect obedience to the Father. He came as Son of man, and as such, was required to walk by faith, just as we are required to do. So, we can look at Jesus and yet see His Father because His whole life was lived in perfect union, obedience, and fellowship with the Father. Because He was the sinless Lamb of God, He was able to do this, something no other man was capable of. He was tempted in all ways, yet without sin. This qualified Him to be our Savior, bear our weakness, become our Bridegroom, and brings us back into oneness with the Father (Isaiah 53).

The next question we might ask is, "Did Jesus drink the cup to marry us?"

The father of the groom then offered the father of the bride, the bride price, and the cup, then he drank and gave the cup to the groom to drink.

Luke 22:41-45 demonstrates the moment that this happened in Christ's marriage to us. *"And He withdrew from them about a stone's throw, and knelt down and prayed saying, "Father, Father, if you are willing, remove this cup from me. Nevertheless, not my will, but yours be done." And being in agony he prayed more earnestly, and his sweat became like great drops of blood falling down to the ground. And when he rose from the prayer, He came to the disciples and found them sleeping in sorrow.* " This was the moment that Jesus not only began to drink the cup to marry us, but also to pay our Mohar, our bride price. Our Bridegroom took the full responsibility for us, His bride, upon His shoulders. Spiritually, physically, and literally, He carried every single aspect of our lives that could ever keep us from Him. He is our faithful Bridegroom.

Our bride price was our sin. He had to pay it to our Father so He could marry us. If not, we would always see ourselves, not in our true Husband's image, but in the image of the one who stole us from our Father's original design. Jesus, being without sin, was the only one who could truly offer our Father the Mohar to pay for our new identity, as He was the only true spotless Lamb whose righteous blood could cover our unrighteousness, making us presentable before our holy God. His blood was our Mohar, our bride price and He paid it in full.

Notice that He drinks before she does. He says to each of us, "I have sealed my commitment to you, even before you say yes to Me. Romans 5:8 affirms this truth, *"But God proves his love for us in this, while we were still sinners, Christ died for us. "*

After He drinks from it, then the daughter is called to give her answer. If she agrees to the marriage, she drinks, and at that point, they are married, as the marriage covenant or B'rit, is fulfilled. At this point, the bride has become a Kallah, an enclosed one, set apart and perfected in her Bridegroom's love and commitment towards her.

He would later veil her; a veil she would continue to wear each time she went out in public. It stood as an outward symbol of an inward promise.

Some scriptures that highlights who we've become once we belong to our Bridegroom can be found in Romans 8:29-30 where it says, *"For those whom he foreknew, he also predestined, to be conformed to the image of his Son, in order that he might be the firstborn among many brothers, and those whom he predestined, he also called, and those whom he called, he also justified, and those whom he justified, he also glorified."*

From the moment that you and I drink from the cup that Jesus, our Bridegroom, has held out to us, God pronounces the words from Matthew 19:6 over us, *"So they are no longer two, but one flesh. What therefore God has joined together let no man separate."*

It's important to note that the promises contained within the Ketubah are the father and son's promises to the bride. Her only response it either to accept or reject these promises. Therefore, the weight of the marriage and the responsibility for upholding it truly rests upon the Bridegroom's shoulders.

And as the groom prepares to leave, he places the gold coin upon his beloved bride's forehead as he veils her, assuring her she is set apart for him. He would say these words to her, in assurance that he would return to fulfill the second portion of the wedding (or the Nissuin), *"And I go to prepare a place for you, I will come again and will take you to myself, that where I am you will be also." (John 14:3).*

We are given everything we need to believe this covenant is secure, as Jesus says to us in John 10:28, *"I give them eternal life, and they will never perish, and no one will snatch them out of my hand."*

From the moment we drink from His cup, we became a whole new being, from our old nature and identity as one tied to an earthly existence in a temporary world, to that of a whole new identity as one with our Savior, Lord and Bridegroom, woven together into a heavenly and eternal existence.

The Mohar, bride price, has been paid in the form of Christ's blood. It must be noted that the amount given for the bride was to be in proportion to what her assumed worth was. When the time to assume our worth came, God gave the only possession He had that would assure us of our worth to Him, not something here on earth as if we are earthly creatures, but He gave His Son's blood. As John 3:16 assures us, *"For God so loved the world that he gave his one and only Son, that whoever believes in Him shall not perish but have eternal life."* I pray we never forget our worth to our Bridegroom and our Lord. We are eternally loved as expressed by God's willingness to secure our way back to Him through the eternal gift of Christ's blood.

Our *Mattan* has been given as the gift of God's Holy Spirit, our guarantee of not only our belonging, but also our reminder of His coming return for us.

As Ephesians 1:13-14 remind us, *"In Him you also, when you heard the word of truth, the gospel of your salvation, and believed in Him, were sealed with a promised Holy Spirit, who is the guarantee of our inheritance until we acquire possession of it, to the praise of His glory"*

And just as the coin was worn on the forehead, so we wear Christ's identity upon our minds as we are transformed into His likeness through this journey of sanctification.

As Revelation 22:4-5 reveals to us, *"They will see His face and his name will be on their forehead.*

There will be no more night. They will not need the light of a lamp or the sun, for the LORD GOD will give them light. And they will reign forever and ever."

As well as Romans 12:2 which says, *"Do not be conformed to this world, but be transformed by the renewal of your mind, that by testing you may discern what is the will of God, what is good and acceptable and perfect."*

Once we become Christ's bride, we can look at all He has given us and know that He has become our justice in this world. And we can live assured that, whatever family, or experiences we have come from, who we are in Him now far exceeds all we might have been through. We are part of a new family, God's family. May He grant us the faith to believe this and apply this to our lives.

I was reminded of this truth as I listened to the testimony of a former prostitute who was dramatically delivered through meeting Christ. She expressed how she tried to leave that lifestyle several times, yet always ended up back because she had an inner belief that she did not belong to herself. As someone who had been sexually abused and exploited most of her life, she did not know how to be in this world apart from under someone else's identity for her. When asked, "how did you finally leave?", her answer touched my heart. She said, "I finally understood that He was really in me, and that I did belong to someone. And even I deserved the life I was giving myself, He didn't."

Her words highlight a truth that is so important for us to understand. Whoever we believe owns us will control us. And an even greater truth is that no one paid for us to belong to God except Jesus.

Therefore, it is important for us to understand who we truly are as His bride. We belong to Him and because we do, are invited to live in His identity here in this world. If we are not experiencing life in His identity for us, we might do well to ask ourselves who we truly belong to.

We have been bought with a price, as 1 Corinthians 6:19-20 assures us, *"Or do you not know that your body is the temple of the Holy Spirit within you, whom you have from God? You are not your own, for you were bought with a price. So glorify God in your body!"*

A few years ago, I bought a picture frame to hold my favorite wedding photo.   The words below the picture read, "All of you, loves all of me." It occurred to me the other day as I glanced at that picture that Jesus is truly the only one in the whole world who can say that and really mean it. When we let Him love us, we get all of Him. And we also get to know true love, love that is intimately acquainted with all of you, and loves you anyway.

We get the honor and privilege of becoming the most loved bride that ever existed, because we are loved by the One who is love.

THE COMMANDMENTS, THE CROSS, AND THE KETUBAH

"But this is becoming is harder than it seems," these lyrics from an old song by Michel W. Smith pop in my head as I begin to write this portion of the study that deals with the wife's part in the wedding. The reason is because I can relate with the words, and I am sure others can too. We live in a world that works completely contrary to who we have become in Christ. While everything around us screams to be more, do more, to become more, Jesus whispers within, "Rest, you are already enough in Me."

In some crazy way, it brings me peace to know that my "becoming" is already complete in Christ. My part is to believe in who He's allowed me to become through His grace. Just as the bride in the ancient Hebrew wedding was left to conform her new identity into her old surroundings, so are we as Christ's bride.

One of the bride's first acts in her new identity was to "unleaven" herself. This means that she would get rid of all her belongings that no longer served her new identity. And the next act which was equally as important was to begin making her wedding dress. This was no easy task as in ancient Hebrew times, fabric was not easy to come by. It often took the bride almost as long to fashion her wedding gown as it took for her groom to build the home they were to live in. As we ponder this truth, let the words from Revelation 19:7-8 pour over you, *"...and the Bride has made herself ready; it was granted her to clothe herself with fine linen, bright and pure-for the fine linen as the righteous deeds of the saints."*

We, as Christ's bride, are given the great call to discover who we've become beyond sin's damaging influence, while at the same time receiving all we are through Christ's righteousness. What we do springs forth from who we've become in Him, weaving a wedding gown over us that is worthy of heaven, an eternal wedding garment, bright and pure. Perhaps the most beautiful aspect of our wedding to Christ is that who we've become is already one with Him, and therefore can never be dissected from Him.

Jesus is the light of the world. And once we become His, we shine with His light because, even though we are still in this world, our inner nature shines with His light through His Holy Spirit in us. Yet, that shine will not show if it's covered up. Just as Jesus said about us in Matthew 5:14-16, *"You are the light of the world. A city set on a hill cannot be hidden. Nor do people light a lamp and put it under a basket, but on a stand, and it gives light to all the house. In the same way, let your light shine before others, so that they may see your good works and give glory to your Father who is in heaven."* As we become unleavened from this world, the light of Christ within us can't help but shine.

We catch a glimpse of this "shine" as we look at Moses, *"as he came down the mountain, Moses did not know that the skin of his face shone because he had been talking with God."* (Exodus 34:29B). As we unbind ourselves from this world and its influence on us and allow God's voice through His Word to become our great illuminator, we shine from the inside out.

Another aspect of this wedding ceremony that I want to note, is the role of the Holy Spirit as matchmaker.

Our matchmaker is the Holy Spirit, who draws us to God and introduces us to Christ. Jesus spoke about Him in John 15:26, *"When the Helper comes, whom I will send to you from the Father, the Spirit of truth, who proceeds from the Father, he will bear witness about me."*

Of course, just as there was an invisible matchmaker for our sake, God also sent a visible matchmaker for the world's sake through John the Baptist.

During ancient times, it was customary to send a servant to the prospective bride's home before the groom showed up. The matchmaker's role was to announce that the groom was coming. We see that John understood his role as Christ's friend and groomsman. John 1:23 clearly portrays him announcing the Bridegroom's (Jesus) coming. *"He said, I am the voice of one crying out in the wilderness. Make straight the way of the Lord'…"* Another scripture that portrays John's role as matchmaker can be found in John 3:22-23 where he announces, *"He who has the bride is the bridegroom. The friend of the bridegroom, who stands and hears him, rejoices greatly at the bridegroom's voice. Therefore, this joy of mine is now complete, He must increase, and I must decrease."*

One of the most important aspects of the wedding is the reading of the wedding contract (the Ketubah). We are familiar with the exchange of vows according to current wedding tradition, however the reading of the Ketubah was very different in that the bride had no vows to offer the bridegroom. Every promise is offered by the groom as he assumes full responsibility for his bride. The Ketubah represented not only a legally binding document, but a religious one as well. This meant that once the bride entered into agreement with her bridegroom, both were legally responsible for all it entailed; the bridegroom for keeping his promises to his bride, and the bride for standing in the promises he made to her and conforming her life to become a recipient of those promises. This covenant follows the pattern of the very first wedding ceremony when Adam stood before his Father, the I Am, and pronounced, *"This at last is bone of my bones and flesh of my flesh; she shall be called Woman because she is taken out of man."* (Genesis 2:23).

This was the birth of marriage, God's invention of bringing one from

two. This was before the Fall, a time when Adam was completely one with God, as no sin had occurred to divide man from God. In essence what Adam is doing is recognizing and giving woman her identify before God, she is bone of his bone, and flesh of his flesh. And the picture of what is truly happening is so profound and beautiful it is almost impossible to describe with words. As bone of his bone, her I am, who she is, is from him, she is fashioned from him and for him. And as he stands before God, he is recognizing her before Him. And because he and God were in perfect alignment, he is able to prophetically call out not only who she is, but what God's creation of marriage is all about, *"Therefore a man shall leave his father and his mother and hold fast to his wife, and the two shall become one flesh. And the man and his wife were both naked and were not ashamed."* *(Genesis 2;24-25).* There is no way he knew, that tucked within these prophetic covenant words, he was telling the story of each of our lives. We will talk more about this in another chapter; however, I just want to take a moment to refer to Paul's words in Ephesians 5:31-32 that echo this truth, *"Therefore a man shall leave his father and mother and hold fast to his wife, and the two shall become one flesh. This mystery is profound, and I am saying that it refers to Christ and the Church."* Just as the first marriage allowed Adam and his wife, Eve, to recognize and enter into God's covenant with them, as both placed their I am into His I AM, as to make one from three, so Christ allows us, His Bride, to come under the same covenant, where we, bone of His bones, enter into Him, placing our I am into His I AM, allowing ourselves to be made one with Him, who left heaven to be joined with us.

Our Ketubah is Christ's new covenant, the B'rit Hadashah, His covenant of blood. We find reference to it in Hebrew 10:15-17 as it says, *"And the Holy Spirit also bears witness to us; for after saying, 'This is the covenant that I will make with them after those days, declares the LORD; I will put My laws on their hearts, and write them on their minds, then He adds, I will remember their sins no more."* Before Christ, our Ketubah was the ten commandments, hence they were written on tablets of stone, representing the peoples' hardness of heart.

Because sin hardened our hearts towards God, rendering us incapable of keeping covenant with Him, He came to earth and gave us His own heart, a heart that carries the full burden of the covenant within it. Paul alludes to our new hearts in 2 Corinthians 3:3 when he says, *"You show that you are a letter from Christ, the result of our ministry, written not with ink, but with the Spirit of the living God, not on tablets of stone, but on tablets of human hearts."*

As we contemplate this truth, we can ask ourselves the question we began with, "what is the wife's part in all of this?" As the husband is given the aggressive part of taking full ownership of his wife's care (physically, emotionally, and spiritually), she is given the submissive role of living in response to him. As we reflect upon her role, we find, tucked within, the true call and identity of the church, His bride. He is the builder of her, and she is keeper of what he is building. She is called to abide in him, just as a rib abides near the heart and lungs, and is, in essence, a keeper to that which life springs from, so we, Christ's bride, are the keeper of His heart and lungs, as we abide in Him. His Spirit and life truly dwell in us, and we are to keep that which He has entrusted within us. Jesus spoke about this in John 15:3-4 when He said, *"Abide in me, and I in you. As a branch cannot bear fruit by itself, unless it abides in the vine, neither can you, unless you abide in me."* And as we abide in Christ, we can "unleaven" ourselves from our former identity which was unable to abide in Christ due to our hardness of heart. As we stay in Christ, we can't help but keep the world out.

CHAPTER
TWO

BECOMING KALLAH

You wake up in the same house, the same bed, to the same sounds and voices, making it easy to assume everything that happened the day before was all just a dream. As if needing tangible evidence to reassure yourself of who you've become, you reach for the coin that was gifted to you by your bridegroom. As you hold it in your hand, memories from the prior day's experiences begin to dance through your mind. *"I have sanctified you to me,"* you can almost hear his voice speaking his promise over you all over again. No longer just Leah, you are now Joseph's Kallah, his secluded one, you are now his bride!

How can this be when everything around you looks the same? Yet, the experience was undeniable, his eyes, his voice, the way he looked at you as he recited his promises. The coins and the veil, your only tangible evidence that these moments really took place. They seem small to you now as you contemplate their huge ramifications. As you prepare for what seems like an ordinary day, you realize that what sets this day apart is that it marks your first day living in your new identity, that of a bride. And because you are a bride, you have a new purpose. Like the sifter you use to separate the husk from the grain, you must now see your life through this new lens as you begin to unleaven yourself from who you've been up until now. You arise a new woman, with a new set of eyes to perceive the world and yourself through. You arise a bride.

The Wait, the Washing, and the Veil

As we just read, the bride's role during her wait is to respond to her new identity as a wife. At first this can seem like a passive approach to her new identity, but nothing can be further from the truth. We will take a little time to unpack more of what the bride is doing as she awaits the return of her bridegroom.

From day one, the bride seeks to make herself beautiful for her groom. Here we can apply scripture to help us better understand what this entails. First Corinthians 13:11 easily applies here, *"When I was a child, I spoke like child, I thought like a child, I reasoned like a child. When I became a man, I gave up childish ways."* This scripture applies to one aspect of the bride's new role in that she has left her childhood season to begin responding to herself and those around her as a woman, as a bride. This indicates not only a change in how she sees herself, but also her responding rightfully from that view regarding how she literally treats her body, her inner beliefs, and her way of being. As she begins to see her body no longer just belonging to her, but also to her husband, she senses a newfound responsibility to care for it in ways that show honor and reverence for her husband, even though she is not physically present with him yet. Some scriptures that help us understand this concept as Christ's bride more readily can be found in 1 Corinthians 6:19-20, *"Do you not know that your bodies are temples of the Holy Spirit, who is in you, whom you've received from God? You are not your own; you were bought with a price. Therefore, honor God with your bodies."* One of the first ways the bride literally carried out this knowledge of her new identify was to take a ceremonial bath in a stream of living water. This act is called Mikvah in Hebrew tradition and it is an act that each Hebrew bride would observe throughout her life as she renewed herself in God's living waters at the end of every menstrual cycle, and after childbirth. It was a way to testifying in her body that she had become a new creation, coming out of a time of being ceremonial unclean (due to the shedding of blood), she was washed in living waters and renewed in God's presence. During Mikvah, the woman is fully immersed in the living waters, making sure that every part of her body is exposed and touched by the cleansing waters. She will flex her fingers and even blink her eyes to ensure every part is touched. There would be a witness with her to bear testimony of her "rebirth."

Our Mikvah is our baptism. Jesus says in John 3:5, *"…Very truly I tell you, no one can enter the kingdom of God unless they are born of water and the Spirit."* Baptism itself does not save us but is an outward expression of the inner Mikvah that has taken place in our heart through the power of the Holy Spirit, just as 1 Corinthians 12:13 assures us, *"For we were all baptized by one Spirit as to form one body-whether Jews or Gentiles, slave or free-and we were all given one Spirit to drink."*

One of the most beautiful expressions we, Christ's bride, get to enjoy in Him is knowing that He is our Mikvah, our Living Water, in whom we can immerse ourselves anytime something in this world comes between His heart and our own. And the immersion not only cleanses us from the outside in, but from the inside out as Jesus says about Himself in John 7:38, *"Whoever believes in me, as Scripture has said, rivers of living water will flow from within them."* Perhaps one scripture that best personifies the oneness Jesus gives us as His bride, is found in Mark 16:16 which states, *"Whoever believes and is baptized will be saved, but whoever does not believe will be condemned."* There is only place that offers living water for full immersion of spirit, soul, and body, leaving us perfectly clean and spotless, and that is Jesus Christ, who was baptized into our death so He might open the Living Way for us.

Another way the new bride would make herself ready was to prepare her trousseau. We found earlier that she would "unleaven" herself from those things that pertained to her old life, however she would also gird herself with those things she would need to step into her new identity. This often includes finding items to carry out her new role as a bride, and to prepare for the wedding day. Brides would usually hand make their wedding dress, and gather the items needed to wait for the wedding day, such as oil for lighting the bride's and bridesmaids' lamp. Each bridesmaid was to carry a well-trimmed lamp because no one knew when the wedding was taking place, not even the bridegroom, but only his father. The well-trimmed lamps symbolized the expectancy and preparation of the bride and her maidens for the wedding day. Jesus told a parable about this in Matthew 25:1-13, *"At that time the kingdom of heaven will be like ten virgins who took their lamps and went out to meet the bridegroom. Five of the virgins were foolish, and five were wise. When the foolish ones took their lamps, they did not take extra olive oil with them. But the wise ones took flasks of olive oil with their lamps. When the bridegroom was delayed a long time, they all became drowsy and fell asleep. But at midnight there was a shout, 'Look, the bridegroom is here! Come out to meet him.' Then all the virgins woke up and trimmed their lamps. The foolish ones said to the wise, 'Give us some of your oil, because our lamps are going out.' 'No,' they replied. 'There won't be enough for you and for us. Go instead to those who sell oil and buy some for yourselves.' But while they had gone to buy it, the bridegroom arrived, and those who were ready went inside with him to the wedding banquet. Then the door was shut. Later, the other virgins came too, saying, 'Lord, lord! Let us in!' But he replied, 'I tell you the truth, I do not know you!' Therefore, stay alert because you do not know the day or the hour."*

Knowing that the unknown hour of the wedding may (and in most cases did) occur at night, the well-trimmed lamps testified of the bride's readiness for her groom's coming. Each night she would place a lamp in her window to attest to her bridegroom that she was ready, she was waiting and that the fire of her heart was burning for him.

The lamps that were often used held small basins for oil that burned up after a while of use. Therefore, there was need for extra oil to ensure the lamp would stay lit during the journey back to the bridegroom's home for the wedding banquet.

This parable is very telling because it not only points to our need to be ready for our Bridegroom's coming, which can only happen if we are connected to our sure source of oil through the Holy Spirit. There are some in the church who live amidst the bride and experience the joy and light that the oil produces yet are not connected to the Source of the oil through the power of the Holy Spirit. Content to stay in proximity to the bride, they neglect the true heart transformation the oil produces.

Did you notice the lamps are lit with olive oil? Our Bridegroom began the pressing to pay for our olive oil in the Garden of Gethsemane, which was literally an olive grove. Those whose lamps will not burn out are ready because they are connected to the oil of the Holy Spirit through receiving Christ Jesus as their Lord and Savior. Those whose lamps will burn out are those who may live in proximity to the bride, and therefore allow themselves to be swayed that close enough is all that's needed.

When Christ comes for His bride, He is looking for one thing, and that is the oil. The oil is evidence that the Holy Spirit is alive and active in His bride. Christ was pressed in the garden, yet able to overcome through submitting to His Father's will. So it is with us, His bride, who united in His same Spirit, will overcome all barriers that keep our hearts from His. Just as a river cannot stop flowing, even if it meets blocks and barriers along the way, so His presence within us is greater and stronger than us, and will not burn out, despite the obstacles we face in our earthly pilgrimage. Those whose oil can succumb to burn out reflect hearts that were not truly connected to Christ who never fails or burns out.

Another way the bride prepared herself during this time was to keep herself veiled or "set apart" as she went out in public. This was her way of declaring to the watching world, "I am hidden within my husband's I am. I may still be present where I was before, but I am EKKLESIA now, I've been called out to live a new existence, even while I am still here in this one." This public testimony was an extension of the moment her bridegroom encompassed her by placing the veil upon her, which will one day be fully realized as the "two become one" during the consummation portion of the wedding which will take place during the second part of the wedding. The bride wore the veil not only to show that she was "called out" in this world, but also to personify her choice of being "called in" to oneness with her beloved bridegroom. The bride sees herself as belonging to her bridegroom and the veil is her way to make public display of this. It takes faith to live the new even as you still dwell in the old. Paul spoke about this aspect of life in Christ in 1 Corinthians 13:12 when he said, *"For now we see in a mirror dimly, but then face to face. Now I know in part, then I shall know fully, even as I am fully known."*

Perhaps the best summary of the bride's role during this portion of the wedding can be summarized in Mark 12:29-31, *"The most important is, hear O Israel: The Lord our God, the Lord is one. And you shall love the Lord your God with all your heart and with all your soul and with all your mind and with all your strength. The second is this, you shall love your neighbor as yourself, there is no other greater commandment than these."* Her realization of who she has become, enables her to live in who she truly is, one with her bridegroom. As we apply this to our role as Christ's bride, we can know that He is real in us and through us, as we tangibly experience His love for us extending beyond us to those around us. Independent of His love, we are not able to love others. Yet, through His, we are loved and extend His love to the world around us. This one portion of Christ's prayer for us found in John 17:26 beautifully testifies to this, *"I have made known to them your name, and I will continue to make it known, that the love with which you have loved me may be in them, and I in them."*

Christ made us one with Him at the Cross and as we each come to Him and accept His acceptance of us, we begin our lifelong journey of realizing who, by His grace, we've become. Before Christ came to marry us, we had no choice about who we would belong to. We were all children of wrath, sinners who did not even have a choice in the matter. But since He has come, there is now a choice. We can accept our new identity as Christ's bride or stay in our old one, disconnected from Love Himself, which leaves us in a constant state of self-protection as opposed to connection with Christ, and through Christ, connection with others.

When we choose to stay in our old identity, it is not God's fault when we reap the consequences of all that identity is tied to. When Christ came to take us as His bride, we were given a choice: would we drink from His cup? Would we be who He has called us to become? Once we choose to become His bride, sin is no longer a way of life for us.

Instead, it becomes a choice we make from our own free will, a will that is choosing to exercise an identity outside of who God enabled us to be.

Sadly, every single one of us will fall back into the traps of our old identity, even after becoming Christ's bride. These traps will often hold us in places we no longer belong, yet are not sure how to emerge from.

Here's the paradox, even this process becomes part of our "unleavening" as we learn to lean into our new identity as Christ's bride instead of falling into our old identity which sought out fleshly and worldly coverings. Just as He promised He would, God works everything for our good as we yearn to truly become His. Sometimes, He allows us to see and acknowledge the truth about ourselves so we can discover our need for Him. One of our greatest struggles is truly knowing and trusting that God made us new when He made us His own. Often, it takes us allowing Him to bring the reality of His light into our darkness before we begin to see the distinction between who we once were, and who He's causing us to become.

These are the moments we are forced to choose to believe, to trust in the reality of Christ's work in us. Until we experience it, we don't truly own it.

Even the act of writing this book is my attempt at doing this very thing. As a woman who has walked through much darkness, and still finds herself all too often aware of my need to "unleaven" myself, it takes some trusting and some believing to continue moving forward towards who I know, by God's grace, I have become through Christ.

It either takes some audacity or some believing to trust that Christ's light within me can shine, despite what I know to be true about myself. Even in writing this, I trust that, *"the light shines in the darkness and the darkness has not overcome it." (John 1:5).*

So, here's your permission, shine anyway!

Shine, not because you have any light to offer, but because He who has truly saved and redeemed you from this dark world, delights to see you truly believing that His light is real in you. This is how you display His oneness with you, and your faith in Him.

Not long ago, I dreamt I was in a dark cave where a big dinner was being held. I was standing next to a young man named Ryan who continued to question my faith in Jesus in a playful, yet intimidating way. As we waited in line for our food, he suddenly became very ill and began to look as if he might die. I ran to get help, but there was no one to help. In desperation, I ran back to Ryan and asked him, "Ryan, can you believe that Jesus is the Lord?" Stunned and weak, he just looked at me as I continued, "Ryan, you are about to die and Jesus is the only one who can save you, you need to confess that Jesus is the Lord!" As those last words came through my mouth, I found myself lifted off the floor as floods of Heavenly light began pouring through me uncontrollably. It was truly as if the words from Isaiah 60:1-2 came to life and were personified in me, *"Arise, shine, for your light has come, and the glory of the LORD has risen upon you. For behold, darkness shall cover the earth, and thick darkness the peoples: but the LORD will rise upon you, and his glory will be seen upon you."*

When I awoke from this dream, I was flooded with awareness of God's holiness and my utter depravity in His presence. Yet, at the same time, I knew it was not because of me or anything I ever did, didn't do or could ever undo that allowed His light to abide in me, it is only Christ's cross that made this possible. Therefore, when I shine with His light, against the backdrop of this dark world, I am proclaiming the reality of all Christ's cross accomplished in me. It's beautiful that He entrusts us with such glory.

On every seed, there is a scar that marks where the seed became detached from its original source. It's our scars that mark where we've detached from God, our original Source. Yet, it's these same scars where Jesus meets us and allows us the most intimate exchange as we find ourselves reattached to Him through His nail print scars. The One who bore all our leaven of sin invites us into such intimate oneness with Him as we reattach to Him with the same wounds that once disconnected us from Him. And at once we find that His oneness with us is as real as His scars. His scars are eternal, and within them, we find that we have a safe place to dwell unleavened from this world.

CHAPTER 3
THE BRIDEGROOM NEARS

You wake up to the soft glow of the lamp burning in the window, a constant reminder to your bridegroom that your heart is ready and waiting on his return for you. Like the oil you must continually maintain to keep the light burning, your heart of expectancy is full and ready to receive your bridegroom. You remember the day you first lit the lamp and placed it in the window almost a year ago, wondering how you would survive the long wait. *The light is still burning for you, my beloved,* are the first thoughts that run through your mind as you take in the hope of a new day, knowing today could be the day – the completion of your wedding day.

It all felt so far off in the beginning, almost like a dream. And yet, since then the same faith it took to light the lamp is manifesting before you as you take in all the ways the promise has become real in your heart, home, and life. Every sense is now engaged in the fruition of this promise; from the scent of the oil burning in the window, to the feel of the linen and lace encompassing you, to the sights and sounds of your bridesmaids who have now become like permanent fixtures as they lay on cots around you. Like you, they are awaiting the sound of the trumpet to call forth, the fulfillment of the wedding to begin. Somehow, within a year your whole life has changed from a girl who once dutifully looked after her family, to a bride awaiting her bridegroom's return. Your heart leaps as you think of how your transformation so mirrors Israel's own.

Israel, a nation called by God as a bride, led forth by His light, awaiting the fulfillment of the moment when her Lord says, *"Arise, shine, for your light has come, and the glory of the LORD has risen upon you."* (Isaiah 60:1)

Just like our father Abraham, we await the fulfilment of the promise, while also walking towards it with our lives. Just as Abraham's promise was fulfilled, you are confident that yours too will be. And like the Shulamite, you will say, *"What is that coming up from the wilderness like columns of smoke, perfumed with myrrh and frankincense, and with all the fragrant powders of a merchant? Behold, it is the liter of Solomon! Around it sixty mighty men of Israel, all of them wearing their swords and expert in war, each with his sword on his thigh, against the terror of night."* (Song of Solomon 3:6-8). And I will rise into the bridal liter and meet my bridegroom in the air, and the two of us will finally become one with our Lord, and with one another.

A Lamp is lit, a Bride Lifted

The second part of the wedding, or the NISIUN (Hebrew word which means to lift) begins when the father of the bridegroom, after close examination of the bridal chamber that the bridegroom has been building since his wedding began, finally determines that it is ready and so he gives the order to his son, "go get your bride!" The father will send a groomsman out before the bridegroom and the other groomsmen to announce, "the Bridegroom cometh!" At this time, the bridegroom will call his groomsmen together, and with torches to light their way, as well as trumpets to announce their coming, they will set out to collect the bride. They will also carry with them a bridal liter or Aperion upon the shoulders. As the trumpets sound, the whole town hears the announcement and everyone who has been invited knows there is about to be a huge, seven-day party they don't want to miss. They will dress in the attire given them by the father of the bridegroom and follow the wedding parade as they join the groomsmen to collect his bride.

At the same time, the bridesmaids and the bride upon hearing the trumpets, will arise, trim their lamps (as this usually occurred at night) and set out to meet the bridegroom party along the way. As the two parties meet, the bride is lifted into the air to be carried in the Aperion upon the shoulders of her bridegroom all the way back to the father's house where a seven-day wedding celebration will take place.

This is where our study takes a prophetic shift as we observe what King Solomon so eloquently wrote about in Song of Solomon 3:6-8, *"What is that coming up from the wilderness like columns of smoke, perfumed with myrrh and frankincense, and with all the fragrant powders of a merchant? Behold, it is the liter of Solomon! Around it sixty mighty men of Israel, all of them wearing their swords and expert in war, each with his sword on his thigh, against the terror of night."* Almost a thousand years before Christ came to the world, King Solomon wrote these words describing a wedding ceremony that you and I as the church will each take part of when we, Christ's bride, will meet Him in the air.

As we wait, we must continually keep in mind that it's not an event we are waiting on, but a person, our Bridegroom Jesus. Because we are not of this world anymore, just as John 17:16 says, *"They are not of the world, just as I am not of the world."*, we must always keep in mind that when Jesus returns, He will be taking up those who have already been lifted in Him and through Him, even while living in this world. As Christ's bride, we've already received an identity that allows us to abide in Him and live above this world. We might even see the rapture as a physical manifestation of a spiritual reality, so that when Christ's bride arises with Him, she will only experience in body what she's already been experiencing in her heart, soul, and spirit all along. We might ask ourselves what this looks like, or how a surrendered bride looks in this world. Well, Mark 12:29-31 may help us see how the lifted life appears, *"The most important is, hear O Israel: The Lord our God, the Lord is one. And you shall love the Lord your God with all your heart and with all your soul and with all your mind and with all your strength. The second is this, you shall love your neighbor as yourself, there is no other greater commandment than these"* This is considered the first and greatest commandment, extending all the way back to the Old Testament. Without a firmly established identity in Christ, this call seems impossible. But our privilege as Christ's bride allows us to enter oneness with Love Himself and helps us to truly love Him and others as only He can. There are moments in my own journey when I am tempted to wonder if I truly am the bride of Christ, yet like a heavenly highlighter reaching down through my heart, He allows me to love someone that I know, in my flesh, is impossible to love except through His love in me. These moments bring such assurance to my heart that I am living the lifted life and that despite my human frailty, Christ is alive and active in me, and His personality overcomes all I am or not.

As we consider this portion of the wedding and how we can live the lifted life, even while still on earth, we must take a moment to look at our Bridegroom, the One who was lifted for our sake. In John 12:32, Jesus says about Himself, *"And if I be lifted up from the earth, I will draw all men unto me."* The Cross is where Jesus truly made Himself one with us, therefore it's the Cross alone that keeps us one with Him. Just as the weight of the bridal liter that carries the bride is placed on the bridegroom's shoulders, and just as the Ark of the covenant was placed on the priest's shoulders alone, so through the Cross, Jesus carried all that ever divided us from Him, as well as all that unites us back to Him. At the Cross, perfect love and holiness collided with the curse that first drove us away from our true identity in Christ. And it's at the Cross our identity as one with God and others is restored. Just as Adam and Eve ate the fruit from the tree of knowledge of good and evil which separated them from God, so through the Cross, we eat from the body and blood of Christ and are united back to Him. Just as He said in John 6:54, *"Whoever eats my flesh and drinks my blood has eternal life, and I will raise them up at the last day."* We even see Adam, just after God announced the curses that will result from he and his wife's disobedience, alluding to this truth as he establishes his wife's name and identity which points to the hope that will one day be fulfilled through God's redemption. *"The man called his wife's name Eve, because she is the mother of all living."* Just as sin entered man through man's rebellion, so sin exits man through one man, Christ's obedience. And just as God carved a woman from the side of man and then offered her to man during the very first marriage, so we, His bride, were taken from the side of Christ at the Cross. Blood and water pouring out from Christ's side, hitting the dirt below, causing an impact so great that the sin-soaked ground rumbled and shook, causing the veil that stood in the temple between God and His bride to be ripped from top to bottom as God's true bride was at last awakened from sin's slumber to hear His words, *"Arise, shine, for your light has come, and the glory of the LORD has risen upon you."* (Isaiah 60:1).

And we, His beloved bride, have been rising ever since. His Holy Spirit within us bears witness to the finished work of Christ. We look at the Cross and ascend, knowing His choice to become One with us completely outweighs anything and everything we do against Him.

I was recently contemplating this very thing while driving home from a grocery trip. As these thoughts wrestled in my mind, I said out loud, "Jesus, how can sin and holiness coexist in the same place?" And at once, my heart heard His answer, "The Cross."

Beloved, He truly did become one with us on the Hill of Calvary. Like a faithful bridegroom, He stood completely vulnerable to love. And just as He was lifted to become one with us, we rise in Him to receive the rest of His finished work over us.

As we abide in Christ's love for us, we allow the world around us to physically see what God's love looks like. Against the dark backdrop of this selfish, sinful world, we shine like lanterns placed in the windows of heaven, welcoming a broken and lost world into the waiting arms of our Father's love.

Our prayer can be, "Lord, take me out while I am in, while I am right here amid the darkness, the chaos, the mundane, the confusion and the pain, take me out right now and seat me in the heavenly places with You, even while my feet still touch the earth." It's easy to become so wrapped up in our fleshly life that we forget we've been crucified to our fleshly lives and are free to fully live in the power we have been given through oneness with our Bridegroom, Jesus.

I have often caught myself calling out to Jesus, "Come Jesus, come down here with me right now!" And He responds, "I already did that. Why don't you come up here with Me." And at once, I can rise in Him, as I experience earthly things grow dim in His presence.

Each time I enter back in, I remember that this is who I am now and the only place I truly belong. Here in His presence, I am already victorious over all that just moments ago threatened to overtake me. In oneness with Him, I stand in His victory, even as my feet still trod this earthly soil. In Him, we are allowed to be taken up and out, even while we are still in. We will not make it any other way. Our only way to stay in love is to literally stay in Him who is love. Christ's love for us is the greatest love story ever, the one from which every other love story merely stands as a shadow in.

In John 19:17, we catch a glimpse of Jesus carrying us, His bride, upon His shoulders, *"So they took Jesus and he went out bearing his own cross, to the place called the place of the skull, which in Aramaic is called Golgotha."* His Cross became our bridal liter, where we are lifted and transformed into oneness with Him. Our humblest and most noble task becomes allowing ourselves to truly be carried in Him.

Not long ago, I was observing my quiet time at our kitchen table and pouring my heart to Jesus in prayer over some painful struggles I was dealing with. What started out as just a few tears turned into great sobs as the feelings of being so alone and misunderstood poured out. As the tears subsided, I noticed the soft music streaming through my radio which I had left on in the other room. These words are what I heard, *"I will rise when He calls my name, no more sorrow, no more pain. I will rise with eagle's wings, before my God, fall on my knees, and rise. I will rise."* (Chris Tomlin, I will Rise). At once, I began to experience myself rising in Christ as I remembered that it is not my circumstances that cause me to get up and keep going, it's the oneness I experience with Christ, my Bridegroom. He gets me up, and in His strength, I rise. No matter what we experience in this life, we can rise, He is our only way up and He is faithful to bear us up no matter what we face.

As we shift our wedding agenda from the first portion, the Kidushin, to the second portion of the wedding, the Nissuin, we must begin to ask ourselves how these portions of the wedding correlates to Christ's marriage to us. We can begin by asking ourselves if Christ is building a home for us in His Father's house. In John 14:2-3, Jesus said, *"In my Father's house are many rooms. If it were not so, would I have told you that I go to prepare a place for you? And if I go and prepare a place for you, I will come again and will take you to myself that were I am you will be also."* We might also ask ourselves if the Father is watching for the completion of this preparation, to let Christ know when it's time to come and take us home to be with Him. In Matthew 24:36, Jesus says about this, *"But concerning the day or the hour, no one knows, not even the angels of heaven, or the Son, but the Father only."*

I don't know about you, but it softens my heart to picture Jesus in heaven right now excitedly awaiting the moment God announces the words He's been waiting to hear as He prepares our heavenly dwelling, "Son, go get your bride!"

To answer the next question which is whether God sent messengers to announce His coming, we must consider that He did this in two ways. One of the messengers He sent was John the Baptist who admitted to being the friend of the Bridegroom in John 3:29, *"The one who has the bride is the bridegroom. The friend of the bridegroom, who stands and hears him, rejoices greatly at the bridegroom's voice. Therefore, this joy of mine is now complete."* The other messenger who announces Christ's coming is the Holy Spirit, who not only calls out to us from within, but also enables us to be used as Christ's vessels. As 2 Corinthians 3:17-18 says, *"Now the Lord is the Spirit, and where the Spirit of the Lord is, there is freedom. We all, with unveiled faces, are looking as in a mirror at the glory of the Lord and are being transformed into the same image from glory to glory; this is from the Lord who is the Spirit."* Other scriptures that support our participation through unity with Christ in calling out to the bride is in Revelation 22:16-17 which says, *"I, Jesus, have sent my angel to testify to you about these things for the churches. I am the root and descendant of David, the bright morning star. The Spirit and the Bride say, "Come." And let the one who hears say, "Come." And let the one who is thirsty come, and let the one who desires take the water of life without price."*

What about the trumpets? Will they sound when your wedding day arrives? Yes, as we see in 1 Thessalonians 4:16, *"For the LORD himself will descend from heaven with a cry of command, with a voice of an archangel and with the sound of the trumpet of God."*

You might also wonder where scripture supports that you will meet your Bridegroom in the air.

1 Corinthians 15:51-53 assures us, *"Listen, I tell you a mystery: We will not all sleep, but we will all be changed—in a flash, in the twinkling of an eye, at the last trumpet. For the trumpet will sound, the dead will be raised imperishable, and we will be changed. For*

the perishable must clothe itself with the imperishable, and the mortal with immortality."

The word *rapturo* is the Greek word meaning "caught up" which is where we get the word rapture. As we look at 1 Thessalonians 4:17, we can find where this word comes from, *"Then we who are alive and remain shall be caught up together with them in the clouds to meet the Lord in the air. And thus, we shall always be with the Lord."* Although there is much debate over when and how the rapture will occur, this book is intended to help us understand not so much about the when and how of the rapture, but about who has come for us. And all He did to ensure that we, His bride, are ready for His coming. As described in the first chapter, when He does appear to receive us to Himself, the rising we experience in that moment will only be an extension of the rising that we have already been experiencing in our Bridegroom through our whole journey within Him here on earth. Just as Ephesians 2:6 assures us, *"And God raised us up with Christ and seated us with him in the heavenly realms in Christ Jesus,"* so we will ever live in the upward call of Christ Jesus. And just as Christ's Spirit in us is alive, active, and abiding in our eternal reality, so will our bodies experience the fulfillment of our destination at the rapture.

CHAPTER 4

THE WISE HAVE OIL
BUT THE FOOLISH
TOIL

You awake with a start as you hear what sounds like a trumpet in the distance. Heart pounding, pulse racing, you leap across the room to strain out your window for a glance. "He's coming!", you cry out as a tsunami of emotions erupt through your body. At once, your small room becomes like a hornet's nest as bridesmaids jump up to prepare you and themselves to meet the parade that is now winding its way towards you. *Today, I will consummate my marriage*, the thought suddenly envelopes you as, with a gulp, you realize the magnitude of what this means. While everyone around you scurries with saris and lamps, your mind is fixed on only one thing, your Bridegroom! Today, you will finally know what it will be like to touch him and to have him touch you. What, by faith you've only imagined at least a million times is now coming to pass.

Today is the day you will ever be with your bridegroom. Who, by faith in his promise, you began becoming over a year ago, you now will ever more be.

Almost on cue, you hear a voice in the distance crying out, "make way, the bridegroom cometh!"

The distant sounds of laughter, cheering, and trumpets blasting only add to the magnitude of joy your heart beats with at this moment.

You grasp the hand of your closest friend, your most faithful bridesmaid and ask her one last time, "how do I look?"

"Like the most beautiful bride!" she retorts as she grabs her lamp and heads for the door.

Like stars shining in the night sky, your lamps dance off the white linen gowns, lighting a path before you and your bridesmaids as you set off to meet the oncoming party. As your feet move forward, you take one last glance back at your family home. Through the veil it appears smaller, almost as if it were merely a cocoon from which you've now emerged to become a whole new creation.

Eyes forward, you are entranced as your senses awaken to the lights, smells, and sounds coming toward you. Like a flower bursting open in Spring, you find your heart already rising within you, ready to receive all the Lord has for you.

A sudden commotion around you breaks through the joy that had just encompassed you. "I have no more oil!", Hanna exclaims in horror as she glances at you.

Eager to move forward, you ask her to run back to town to buy some more from a nearby merchant. To come to the party with an untrimmed lamp was not an option as it would be a huge insult to the father of the bridegroom who has spared no expense to provide everything needed for the bride and her bridesmaids to celebrate this momentous occasion for seven whole days. "I'll be right back! Don't shut the door without me," she calls as she runs back to the place you just emerged from.

THE REALIZATION AND THE RESPONSIBILITY

There is a relationship that is required once we begin walking with Christ, yet not always understood. It is the relationship that exists between realizing we are the bride and the responsibility of our new identity. Easier to see within the context of an earthly marriage, we seldom place the same emphasis on our spiritual marriage to Christ. For instance, how many of us have ever attended a wedding where the bride was half dressed, or only partially ready? Most weddings I have been a part of involves the bride spending at least the entire day, if not the entire week, preparing for her trip down the aisle. We can assume the reason the bride takes such care to present herself ready for such a joyous occasion is because she not only believes she is the bride, but she also allows the reality of who she's become to inform her actions to prepare herself. Therefore, we could assume that the bride takes responsibility for appearing ready for her wedding day because she realizes she is the bride. It's her realization that brings her to take responsibility for making herself ready for her wedding day.

This may sound simplistic as we compare a bride rightly ready for her wedding day as the bride of Christ, however if the wedding shoe fits, we ought to wear it.

I remember my own wedding day, crowded in a large, yet busting at the seams church bathroom, my bridesmaids and I made our last-minute preparations for the walk we were about to take down the aisle. One of my bridesmaid's had not altered her dress and therefore wasn't ready and so, like buzzing bees around her, older ladies from the church were scrambling around her trying to get her dress pinned well enough to make it through the ceremony. Caught up in the bustle of all that was happening around her, I almost forgot for a moment that it was my wedding day.

I remember looking up into the mirror and realizing that I hadn't finished my make-up and had only minutes left before the wedding was to begin.

The sense of urgency swept over me as I knew I had to focus all my attention on getting myself ready to walk down the aisle to meet my husband.

There comes a moment in each of our lives when we must stop looking at others to see if they are ready for the wedding, and instead begin to look into the mirror of our own heart to make sure we are ready. In Matthew 25:1-13, Jesus tells a parable about a wedding in which some of the bridesmaids were not ready when the wedding came. This parable not only helps us catch glimpses of an ancient Hebrew wedding, but more importantly it helps us search our own heart to ensure we are ready for His coming. The parable goes like this:

"Then the kingdom of heaven will be like ten virgins who took their lamps and went to meet the bridegroom. Five of them were foolish, and five were wise. For when the foolish took their lamps, they took no oil with them, but the wise took flasks of oil with their lamps. As

the bridegroom was delayed, they all became drowsy and slept. But at midnight there was a cry, 'Here is the bridegroom! Come out to meet him.' Then all those virgins rose and trimmed their lamps. And the foolish said to the wise, 'Give us some of your oil, for our lamps are going out.' But the wise answered, saying, 'Since there will not be enough for us and for you, go rather to the dealers and buy for yourselves.' And while they were going to buy, the bridegroom came, and those who were ready went in with him to the marriage feast, and the door was shut. Afterward the other virgins came also, saying, 'Lord, lord, open to us.' But he answered, 'Truly, I say to you, I do not know you.' Watch therefore, for you know neither the day nor the hour."

In this parable we find that all the bridesmaids became drowsy and slept because the bridegroom was taking too long. As we were just referring to above, the bride's greatest responsibility as bride is to realize who she has become. Because the bride believes she truly has become the bride, no person or circumstance can convince her otherwise. She is wise and is ready when her bridegroom comes for her because she believes herself to be the bride, she has taken responsibility for her identity as the bride. Even before her bridegroom appears, she has operated in His new identity for her, which enables her to not only keep her lamp full, but to have an abundance of oil left over. On the other hand, the foolish virgin only has enough oil for a few hours and then her light goes out and she finds herself in a predicament. She asks the other bridesmaids for oil, but they let her know they cannot give her their oil lest they not have enough for the journey ahead.

The lamps during Jesus' time were small and made from clay, they held a reservoir for enough olive oil to keep the lamp lit for about four hours. Because the journey to the wedding might take hours or in some cases, even a day or two, there was need for extra oil to keep the lamps lit.

As we consider this parable and the implications for us, His bride, when we do not have enough oil, we might consider this portion of the wedding as our "one last glimpse in the mirror" before meeting our Bridegroom Jesus.

In the Bible, olive oil represents the Holy Spirit given to us upon our profession of faith and reception of our new life in Christ. Romans 8:9-11 clearly indicate that we are given God's Holy Spirit to live within us and to be led by once this new life in Christ begins.

The scriptures say, *"You, however, are not in the flesh but in the Spirit, if in fact the Spirit of God dwells in you. Anyone who does not have the Spirit of Christ does not belong to him. But if Christ is in you, although the body is dead because of sin, the Spirit is life because of righteousness. If the Spirit of him who raised Jesus from the dead dwells in you, he who raised Christ Jesus from the dead will also give life to your mortal bodies through his Spirit who dwells in you."*

Just as a bride takes responsibility for her new identity, so we, Christ's bride are to take responsibility for living out His identity within us. Because we have died to the flesh we once lived in, we are free to live fully through His Holy Spirit which offers us limitless oil with which to make our way towards Him faithfully for all our lives.

Consider this your opportunity to truly examine your heart and ask yourself whether you are really living in the Holy Spirit? If so, you are standing in oneness with Christ and in His righteousness, you not only have enough, but you are enough. Because your flesh has died with Him, you will not only rise with Him at His coming but are already rising with Him even while you await your union with Him.

There is danger in thinking where we are in Christ is enough. Like the foolish virgins who ran out of oil and begged the others for some of theirs, there will be those standing with us in the church who do not have enough oil to enter in when Christ comes. They were trusting that they had enough as opposed to allowing Christ to become their enough. If we go back to the beginning when the very first wife was procured from the side of her husband, we can catch a glimpse of the difference between brides who have enough oil and those who don't.

Genesis 2:22-25, *"And the rib that the LORD God had taken from the man he made into a woman and brought her to the man. Then the man said,*

"This at last is bone of my bones   and flesh of my flesh;she shall be called Woman,   because she was taken out of Man. Therefore, a

man shall leave his father and his mother and hold fast to his wife, and they shall become one flesh. And the man and his wife were both naked and were not ashamed."

As we look at the very first bride that God made, we can see that she originates from her husband, Adam. She is taken and formed from within Him. We could say that she even existed in him before she was created from him. As it was with her, so it is with us, Christ's bride. We are held in Him, therefore we have limitless supply from Him. We find Paul affirming this truth in 2 Timothy 1:6-9 where it says, *"For this reason I remind you to fan into flame the gift of God, which is in you through the laying on of my hands, for God gave us a spirit not of fear but of power and love and self-control. Therefore do not be ashamed of the testimony about our Lord, nor of me his prisoner, but share in suffering for the gospel by the power of God, who saved us and called us to[a holy calling, not because of our works but because of his own purpose and grace, which he gave us in Christ Jesus before the ages began, and which now has been manifested through the appearing of our Savior Christ Jesus, who abolished death and brought life and immortality to light through the gospel,"*

We see from the scriptures above that not only is the Spirit in us, but that we've been called in Christ before the ages even began. We also see here that we are encouraged to take responsibility to "fan into flame," the gift that God has given us.

It is not so with those who might identify as the bride, yet do not exist in Him. We see Christ affirming this in Matthew 7:21-23, *"Not everyone who says to me, 'Lord, Lord,' will enter the kingdom of heaven, but the one who does the will of my Father who is in heaven. On that day many will say to me, 'Lord, Lord, did we not prophesy in your name, and cast out demons in your name, and do many mighty works in your name?' And then will I declare to them, 'I never knew you; depart from me, you workers of lawlessness.'"* The word for knew used here means recognize or realize. It's a fearful thing to think Jesus would not acknowledge us, even those of us who claim to acknowledge Him. Yet, we've all known those who claim to be married, yet somewhere along the way, stopped acknowledging the one they vowed to be united with.

As humans prone to sin, left to ourselves, we revolve around ourselves and expect others to as well. Yet in Christ, we are not only welcomed into Him, but He makes His home in us, so that we are free to revolve around Him, and by doing so, we allow His identity to be expressed through us, therefore becoming recognizable to the world. Some of the most profound moments in my life have taken place when I discovered the reality of Jesus in me as I found myself responding to people or situations as He would, not in the way I typically would if left on my own. If we are truly One with Christ, we should be able to look at our lives now and literally see evidence of His life within us, not what we perceive to be evidence, but true evidence of His love, mercy, and grace poured through our lives. We should experience His peace within our hearts, especially at times when we know we have no business feeling peace. Like David says in Psalm 23:6, we can look back at our lives and say, *"surely, goodness and mercy have followed me all the days of my life, and I shall dwell in the house of the LORD forever."*

If this is not our Christian experience, whether we are in church or even in ministry, we must look into the mirror of our hearts and ask if we are truly one with Christ. What mercy He extends to us to allow us more time to truly examine our hearts so we can realize the truth about ourselves and make the adjustments necessary to truly become His beloved bride.

Many years ago, I was attending a women's conference where I was asked to speak in front of a group of women attendees. Because these women were in ministry, I felt very intimidated and wanted to impress them. As I prepared my speech and sought to memorize every part of it so I could appear polished and put together, I could sense that still small voice nudging me, and I knew Jesus was convicting my heart.

I could sense Jesus asking my heart, "Rhonda, where are you?"

And although I didn't want to acknowledge what my answer was, I knew unless I was in Him, nothing I said, no matter how impressive, would impact anyone. As I set my well-worn notes aside to listen to His instruction for me, I knew He was asking me to let go of who I wanted to be and how I wanted to appear in front of others, and instead, stand in Him, fully trusting in His power to shine through me.

I am so thankful for that moment and that it happened before I ever published a Bible study or spoke to a group of women. I am thankful that before I ever tried to build a platform to stand on so others could see me, He taught me to instead stand upon the only platform He ever called any of us to, the Cross. As I look back over my life in serving Him and following Him, it looks very different from where I once believed it was headed. Yet, I recognize Jesus along the way, and my heart delights to see His trail of goodness and mercy following me. I stand in full confidence that I have become His bride, bone of His bones, flesh of His flesh, taken out of His side and being led forth until I stand at His side forevermore.

Chapter 5

The Rapture and the Enraptured

Your heart pounds wildly as the parade of activity heading towards you and your bridesmaids come into full view. Shouts of joy, laughter and singing becomes louder, mixing with the shimmers of light from the censors and lamps bouncing off the Aperion heading towards you. Like a parade where joy is the theme, you find yourself caught up in the majestic wonder of your wedding day. Before joining your groom in the bridal liter, you realize your heart has already lifted into the joyful abyss before you. Filled with wonder, you sing along with those coming towards you. Your bridesmaids join you as the two becoming one manifests into the atmosphere. One song, one spirit, one joy bursts forth through the dark night, overcoming it as it reaches towards heaven, a divine proclamation that what God began in heaven is now being fulfilled here on earth. The bride and groom He brought together are at last becoming one. *"What God has joined together, let no man separate." (Mark 10:9)*

Taken Up Inside, In the Bridegroom I Hide

It begins with music, the trumpets blasting as the beat of the drums, and shaking tambourines and joyful singing permeates the night sky with sounds of celebration. The time has come, the bride has made herself ready, the bridal chamber complete, and the bridegroom's father has granted his permission to bring home the bride. The music, drifting through the windows and doorways of everyone in the surrounding villages, calls out the invitation to join the joyful celebration of the bride and bridegroom, and celebrate their individual identity as the beloved bride of God. Surely, the words from Isaiah 54:5 rang out in remembrance to everyone present, *"For your Maker is your husband-*

the LORD of hosts is his name; and the Holy One of Israel is your Redeemer, the God of the whole earth he is called." Even the lamp lights and torches, blazing through the night point to the wedding story planned from the beginning of creation, the story of God's love and light, bursting through the darkness and overcoming it. *"The people who walk in darkness will see a great light; Those who live in a dark land, The light will shine on them." (Isaiah 9:2).*

Only God's people are chosen as both bride and bridesmaid, and each wedding is a reminder of the privileged position we hold as God's children.

As the Aperion draws nearer to the bridal party, the joy and tension reaches near crescendo. Soon the bride will meet her beloved in the air, and what began nearly a year ago as a covenant of faith, becomes a reality of sight, sound, taste, and touch. Truly faith will have become sight.

The words from Song of Solomon 2:10 personifies the lifting of the bride to join her bridegroom in the Aperion. *"...Arise, my love, my beautiful one and come away."*

After the bride is collected, the party heads back to the father of the bridegroom's house to begin the seven-day wedding celebration. The Nissuin, or home-taking, has begun. The second part of the wedding is in full swing.

This is where our wedding ceremony takes a more prophetic swing as we, Christ's bride, catch glimpses of what will be. Just as the bride and bridal party prepare for the home-taking, so do we. When the lifting of our bodies from earth to heaven occurs, it will be an extension of how we've lived in Christ on earth. The Rapture is taken from the Latin word "rapio" which means caught up, as used in 1 Thessalonians 4:17, *"After that, we who are still alive and are left will be caught up together with them in the clouds to meet the Lord in the air. And so, we will be with the Lord forever."* For those of us who live here and now by the Spirit of the Living God, in that moment, we will become all we've believed ourselves to be during our earthly journey.

Our faith will become our sight, and we will see the One in whom we've been standing this whole time. The rapture of the Church will mark an eternal beginning for each of us standing in Christ, as well as the beginning of the end for those left in this world. Just as those who celebrated their identity as God's chosen ones longed to attend the weddings of those who were joining in marriage, not only as an opportunity to enter their joy, but also to be reminded of their identity in Christ. So also those who did not attend were in essence marking their unwillingness to embrace God's invitation to identify as His bride.

This distinction will take place when Christ's bride, the Church, is raptured from the world. Like a bright, neon, heavenly highlighter, God will clearly mark His sovereign authority upon the world, leaving no doubt that He is Lord. The question of whether God truly knows our hearts will be answered in a way that provides the whole world to witness His truth and His ability to distinguish His true children in this world.

"For the mystery of lawlessness is already at work. Only he who now restrains it will do so until he is out of the way." (2 Thessalonians 2;7). With the restrainer of the Holy Spirit lifted from the world, the world will be set to experience God's wrath upon those who refused to enter in. Just as God shut the door to Noah's Ark, so also the door of salvation through grace will be closed to those who refused to become His and be delivered from the wrath to come. Christ is our only door to life in this world, as 1 Corinthians 15:22-24 says, *"For as in Adam all die, so also in Christ shall all be made alive. But each in his own order; Christ the first fruits, then at his coming those who belong to Christ. Then comes the end, when he delivers the kingdom to God the Father after destroying every rule and every authority and power."* Unless we are abiding in Christ, we have no access to life and are therefore, like Adam, staying in subjection to this dying world. One day, the world will be forced to look into God's mirror to see the truth about herself, that she has chosen death by not taking advantage of God's gift of life through Christ's sacrifice on the Cross.

1 Corinthians 15:49-54 goes on to say about this moment of clarity that will soon come upon the whole world, *"Just as we have borne the image of the man of dust, we shall also bear the image of the man of heaven. I tell you this brothers, flesh and blood cannot inherit the kingdom of God, nor does the perishable inherit the imperishable. Behold! I tell you a mystery. We shall not all sleep, but we shall all be changed, in a moment, in the twinkling of an eye, at the last trumpet. For the trumpet will sound, and the dead will be raised imperishable,*

and we shall be changed. For this perishable body must put on the imperishable, and this mortal body must put on immortality. When the perishable puts on the imperishable, and the mortal puts on immortality, then shall come to pass the saying that is written: 'Death is swallowed up in victory.' 'O death, where is your victory? O death, where is your sting?'"

For those of us wearing the imperishable identity granted through Christ's atonement on the cross, there will be a moment when what we've always worn on the inside suddenly bursts forth to the outside. The new creation we've become in Christ will become fully visible as the victory Christ won over death fully extends to His bride. The words from Isiah 54:5 will become our reality, *"For your Maker is your husband—the LORD of hosts is his name; and the Holy One of Israel is your Redeemer, the God of the whole earth he is called."*

Once the shofar sounds, the bride's time of preparation is over, her day has come, and she will fully step into her identity.

In light of His coming at any moment for us, there is a temptation for us to busy ourselves with kingdom work as a way to prepare for our Bridegroom's coming. There is something about tangibly doing something that helps us feel more in control. Yet, Matthew 7:21-23 says, *"Not everyone who says to me, 'Lord, Lord.' will enter the kingdom of heaven, but the one who does the will of my Father who is in heaven. On that day many will say to me, 'Lord, Lord, did we not prophesy in your name, and cast out demons in your name, and do many mighty works in your name? And then will I declare to you, 'I never knew you; depart from me, you workers of lawlessness,'"* we are wise to consider that Jesus would have His bride abiding in Him, therefore the works extending from His bride originate from Him, as opposed to her own ideas about Him or what she feels He might want. In other words, He's coming for a being bride, not just a doing bride.

A bride that is truly abiding in Him cannot help manifesting Him through her life. The Greek word knew in the above verse is Ginosko, it means approving connection or realize. It is an action word; however, the action cannot be disassociated from the one with whom the connection is realized. To think about the Rapture is sobering because it represents finality, a moment in time when God closes the door. How we respond to this knowing reveals the level of our readiness. Christ's bride is ready because her heart is fully resting on the One who came for her. She is concerned less and less about what she sees with her eyes, and more and more about who she has become through His eyes. For the bride, she can truly say, "my maker is my husband," because all she has become came through His responsible care for her.

As I struggled to discern if I was truly abiding in Christ as His bride, or merely my own understanding of myself as His, I was led to an experience that helped me catch a glimpse of the difference. My husband's work offered us the chance to take a trip on a zip line tour. I am a little scared of heights but did not want to miss out on the opportunity to catch glimpses of the beauty that surrounded us. Linked from strong, metal cables that hung above us, I felt secure as we made our way through the narrow cat walks that stretched across the mountainous terrain surrounding us, yet there came the moment when I reached the first launch pad from which I was to jump from my only sure place to stand in the flatform beneath me. As I neared the edge, I knew I was going to do it, but I didn't know how to let my feet leave the spot I was now standing. Frozen in fear and apprehension, the guide instructed me to simply sit back and let the weight of my body fully rest in the cable above me. I began to feel the tension shift from my body onto the cord that now held me fully, and to my shock and amazement, I began to fly forward. Not a jump, simply a rest, and I was carried fully to the other side.

As I made my way across, I became suddenly aware that this is what faith tangibly looks like, transferring all my weight upon God's ever ready hands holding me, and knowing He surely will carry through to the other side. Life has thrown me more than a few curve balls since that day, yet I find that as I rest fully on the One to whom I belong, I am continually amazed by how faithfully Jesus carries me forward to the next place to stand as I catch glimpses of Him that I surely would have missed had I not allowed Him to carry me. In this way, even before the rapture comes, I am continually enraptured by His love and my ability to experience His love and care for me, even before I see Him face to face. His ever-approving connection to me is manifested when I take Him up on His offer to be made one with Him. It's a connection that I can never be disconnected from because it is not secured by me, but by my Bridegroom, Jesus. *"What therefore God has joined together, let not man separate." (Mark 10:9).*

CHAPTER 6

DRESSED AS A
KING, HE MAKES
AWAY FOR HIS
QUEEN

Before your eyes lift to meet his, you first notice the kittel he is wearing, a gift you sent over a few months ago in anticipation of this day. Dressed in the robes you wrapped for him endears your heart to him even more as you realize before you even entered the Aperion he was already dressed in that which attaches him to you. The two had already become one and now your eyes are only beginning to see the full manifestation of it. As he reaches for you to steady you in the bridal liter, you notice how his hand is shaking. Nervous laughter spills through your lips as you grab his hand, and at last touch your bridegroom for the very first time since the day he departed to prepare a place for you. As you hold his hand, you can't help but imagine that these are the hands that will hold you for the rest of your life. He is more handsome than you remembered. Emotions you never knew existed spill out from you like a mysterious concoction. You are thankful for the fanfare exploding all around you, a pleasant distraction from the volcano erupting inside you. Dressed like a king, you find yourself bathed in new awareness of who you've become as his bride, a queen, an ambassador before God to represent to this world the beauty of His splendor, the majesty of His love, and His sovereignty over His people. Like the crown formed into the shape of Jerusalem's walls that has just been placed on your head by your bridegroom, you feel the weight of all God's allowed you to become. *"You shall be a crown of glory in the hand of the LORD, and a royal diadem in the hand of your God. You shall no longer be termed Forsaken, nor shall you your land any more be termed Desolate; but you shall be called Hephzibah (My delight is in Her), and your land*

Beulah (Married); for the LORD delights in you, and your land shall be married." (Isaiah 62:3-4) Although this is your wedding day, it also belongs to Him and everything about this union points back to Him who not only created the first man and woman, but also created the covenant of marriage. *"It is not good for man to be alone; I will make him a helper suitable for him."* (Genesis 2:18). The weight of these words sink deeply into you, causing your stomach to knot up and tears to sting your eyes as you contemplate God's favor and mercy towards you in allowing you to take part in extending His creation. One day, this union you are entering into will bear fruit for Him and so His love story for His people will continue to march through this world, leaving the undeniable trail of His marks upon every person to see and know that He, alone is God.

In modern weddings, all eyes are on the bride, yet it was not so in the ancient Hebrew wedding. The true star of every ancient Hebrew wedding was God and His role as creator. Because each wedding celebrated God's continued faithfulness in fulfilling and keeping His covenant to His people, therefore every aspect of the wedding tradition pointed back to Him in some way, including what the bride and bridegroom wore.

The groom was dressed like a king on his wedding day, this alludes not only to Song of Songs where the bridegroom is likened to a king, such as in Song of Solomon 1:4 where it says, *"Draw me after you; let us run. The king has brought me into his chamber."*, but also to Psalm 45, where a description of a Hebrew bridegroom is portrayed as a king. As we will soon see, both paint pictures of Christ, our Bridegroom and King. Although dressed like a king, the bridegroom wore a kittel, or plain, linen, jacket that carried small fringes around the bottom edge, over his kingly attire.

The kittel was often a gift from his bride, presented to him in anticipation of his coming for her. The kittel first worn on his wedding day, would become part of the attire he would wear each religious holiday thereafter. Lastly, he would be buried in it. It held no pockets to symbolize that one marries for love, not money, and to symbolize the fact that we come with nothing into this world, and so will we leave. The kittel is worn as a reminder of our mortality, that this life must be carefully lived with one's departure from this world in mind. Because the Hebrews are God's chosen people and He is an everlasting God, the wedding became a time to reaffirm the truth that our lives here on earth are merely a portal through which we will enter eternal life with God. The bridegroom would be assisted by his groomsmen when putting on the kittel for two reasons, first, because he is to be treated as a king on his wedding day who does not dress himself. And second, because, again, he is to keep in mind that he will wear this same garment on the day of his burial, when he again, will be dressed by his attendants. The kittel symbolized a prayer that is proclaimed on the wedding day that, *"love is as strong as death." (Song of Solomon 8:6)*. There are thirty-two fringes on the kittel, which are symbolic for the Hebrew word heart.

From the moment the groom goes to receive his bride, he fasts to keep himself fully free and aware of the covenant he is fulfilling. He won't eat or drink until after he has been made fully one with his beloved bride.

Once the bridegroom and bride return to the father's house, the bridegroom will immediately be escorted into the groom's reception. He would have a table set before him with food and drink and seated at the table with him would be his father, the bride's father, and several rabbis. Beyond that, the groom's male friends and relatives would be there to toast and sing in celebration of their friend's wedding day. The groom, who would not partake of the food or drink, would await the most sobering moment when the ketubah, or marriage contract, is reviewed by the rabbis. Once found to be ceremonial sound, the groom will formally accept the obligations of the ketubah by executing a *kinyan sudar,* a traditional legal consent and agreement process in which the groom is handed a handkerchief by one of the attending rabbis. The bridegroom will lift the handkerchief in the air, in front of witnesses, before returning it to the rabbi.

WEARING OUR MESS TO PURCHASE OUR DRESS

Even as we consider the attire of the bridegroom on his wedding day, how was our Bridegroom, Jesus, dressed?

Was He dressed as a King? Matthew 27:27-31 gives us a glimpse of our Bridegroom on His wedding day, *"Then the soldiers of the government took Jesus into the governor's headquarters, and they gathered the whole battalion before him. And they stripped him and put a scarlet robe on him, and twisting together a crown of thorns, they put it on his head and put a reed in His right hand. And kneeling before him, they mocked him saying, 'Hail King of the Jews!' And they spit on him and took the reed and struck him on the head. And when they had mocked him, they stripped him of the robe and put his own clothes on him and led him away to crucify him".* Note that the above scriptures affirm Jesus was dressed by others on His wedding day. John 19: 1-2 also gives us another glimpse of this portion of the wedding being fulfilled, *"Then Pilate took Jesus and flogged him. And the soldiers twisted together a crown of thorns and put it on his head and arrayed him in a purple robe."*

There is something here that we might miss without taking a closer look at the crown that was placed upon His head. In Genesis 3:17-18 we find a curse handed down to Adam by God just after the Fall, *"And to Adam he said, because you have listened to the voice of your wife and have eaten from the tree of which I commanded you "You shall not eat of it" cursed is the ground because of you, in pain you shall eat of it all the days of your life: thorns and thistles is shall bring forth for you."* As we consider the crown that Jesus wore as He became one with us, His bride, we cannot miss that the crown He bore directly points back towards the curse handed down to humankind at the Fall. He literally wore our curse upon His head. Isaiah 53:4-5 portrays our Bridegroom bearing the curse on our behalf, *"Surely, he has borne our griefs and carried our sorrows; yet we esteemed him stricken, smitten by God, and afflicted. But he was pierced for our transgressions; he was crushed for our iniquities; upon him was the chastisement that brought us peace, and with his wounds we are healed."* A curse handed down to man who decided to become a self-sovereign as opposed to resting in his Creator's sovereign love for him. We, who decided to become our own kings, deserve to be cut off from the One whom we disobeyed because He is holy, and sin must be dealt with. But because God is love, He can't let us go without loving us to the end. Perhaps we catch the most profound picture of Jesus portraying both His love and His Kingship over us in John 19:5 when, after receiving the stripes through which we are healed, Jesus is asked to stand in the praetorium before the people who only one week before hailed Him as their Messiah, yet now want to see Him crucified. *"So, Jesus came out, wearing a crown of thorns and a purple robe. Pilate said to them, "Behold the man!"* *"Behold the man,"* how I pray we take time to truly see the full implication of these words. This is the One of whom it is said in Colossians 1:19, *"For in him all the fullness of God was pleased to dwell."* The fullness of God fully expressing the perfect balance of love and mercy because only He can. *"Out of the anguish of his soul he shall see and be satisfied; by his knowledge shall the righteous one, my servant make many to be accounted righteous."* (Isaiah 53:11). Our bridegroom came for us and became king over all that might separate our hearts from Him. In Genesis 3:16, we see another aspect of the curse, this one handed to Eve just after the Fall, *"Your desire shall be for your husband and he shall rule over you.*" At the Cross, Jesus offered every one of us who is willing to receive Him, a husband in whom our hearts are completely safe to let rule us. Let our prayer be to desire our beloved husband, Jesus, under whose rule we are afforded life and love eternal.

Now that we know He was dressed as a king, did Jesus wear a kittel? Matthew 27:58-59 gives a glimpse of what Jesus wore as He lay in the tomb on His wedding day, *"He went to Pilate and asked for the body of Jesus. Then Pilate ordered that it be given to him. And Joseph took the body and wrapped it in a clean linen shroud and laid it in his own new tomb"* Although we can't know for sure whether this clean linen shroud was a kittel, we do know from scripture that Jesus was dressed by another on His wedding day, and that He was buried in linen.

What about the groom's reception where the ketubah is ratified? Did this take place for Jesus?   Luke 22:14-20 gives us a glimpse into Jesus' last moments with His groomsmen before fully becoming one with us, His bride. *"And when the hour came, he reclined at table, and the apostles with him. And he said to them, "I have earnestly desired to eat this Passover with you before I suffer. For I tell you I will not eat it until it is fulfilled in the kingdom of God." And he took a cup, and when he had given thanks he said, "Take this, and divide it among yourselves. For I tell you that from now on I will not drink of the fruit of the vine until the kingdom of God comes." And he took bread, and when he had given thanks, he broke it and gave it to them, saying, "This is my body, which is given for you. Do this in remembrance of me." And likewise the cup after they had eaten, saying, "This cup that is poured out for you is the new covenant in my blood."* We see from these scriptures reference to Jesus fasting, as well as His reference to the new covenant, the covenant of grace by which we are reconciled into fellowship with God through the redemption Christ fulfilled for us at the Cross. It's through this covenant that we become one with Christ and are afforded the new identity as His bride.

What about the kinyan sudar, a traditional legal consent and agreement process in which the groom is handed a handkerchief, was it given? We find our answer to this in John 20:3-9 where it says, *"So Peter went out with the other disciple, and they were going toward the tomb. Both of them were running together, but the other disciple outran Peter and reached the tomb first. And stooping to look in, he saw the linen cloths lying there, but he did not go in. Then Simon Peter came, following him, and went into the tomb. He saw the linen cloths lying there, and the face cloth, which had been on Jesus' head, not lying with the linen cloths but folded up in a place by itself. Then the other disciple, who had reached the tomb first, also went in, and he saw and believed; for as yet they did not understand the Scripture, that he must rise from the dead."* The word used for face cloth in this scripture is the Greek word, sudarium, which means handkerchief or head scarf. It was Jewish custom to wrap the face of a deceased in such a cloth. We see this same word used when describing the cloth around Lazarus' face in John 11:44 where it says, *"The man who had died came out, his hands and feet bound with linen strips, and his face wrapped with a cloth." Jesus said to them, "Unbind him, and let him go."* The word "folded" found in John 20:7 in many Bible translations also gives readers the impression that the "sudarium" was folded like one would fold his handkerchief or a towel. There is so much to unpack here as we make correlations to an ancient Hebrew wedding with that of Jesus marriage to us, the church and bride. First, we notice that when Lazarus was resurrected, he came out bound, hence Jesus' command to, *"unbind him and let him go."* We can assume that Jesus was resurrected unbound as the linen strips were lying right where he was placed in the tomb, with only the face cloth set apart and folded. Not only that, but there was some thoughtfulness in the way Jesus left the handkerchief that had covered His face, folded, and apart from the other burial clothes. To truly unpack the importance of this detail we must discover more fully what takes place during a *kinyan sudar.* First, in order for the binding agreement to be made, the "kerchief" must legally belong to the one presenting it. There are to be two witnesses present during kinyan. In the presence of the two witnesses, the bridegroom, lifts the kerchief at least ten inches as a way of expressing that he received the commitment, that he's received his bride. The kerchief is then handed back to its owner. The idea is that, in lifting the kerchief, the bridegroom is taking it unto himself, or assuming responsibility for the one the kerchief represents, in this case, his bride. We can assume that when Jesus resurrected and sat or stood up, the kerchief was lifted at least ten inches into the air. We also know from scripture that there were two witnesses present with Jesus in the form of two angels as shown in scripture in John 20:11-12 where it says, *"But Mary stood weeping outside the tomb, and as she wept she stooped to look into the tomb. And she saw two angels in white, sitting where the body of Jesus had lain, one at the head and one at the feet."* Besides the witness of the angels, within Christ Himself are the witness of the Father and the Holy Spirit as affirmed in both John 10:30, *"I and the Father are one."* (Jesus), and 2 Corinthians 3:17, *"Now the Lord is the Spirit, and where the Spirit of the LORD is there is freedom."* In the case of Christ fulfilling His marriage covenant to us, we find the kerchief left, and neatly folded, an expression that the responsibility has been taken fully on the part of our Bridegroom Jesus, and now the kerchief, neatly folded in a place by itself symbolizes the opportunity for any one of us who is willing, to enter the marriage covenant that He has so freely secured for us. One of the last scriptures in the Bible echoes this invitation in Revelation 22:17, *"The Spirit and the Bride say, "Come." And let the one who hears say, "Come." And let the one who is thirsty come; let the one who desires take the water of life without price."*

Our last look at what is worn on our wedding day deals with what we, His bride are to wear. Ephesians 5;25-32 allows us a glimpse of how we are to appear as Christ's bride. Although these scriptures refer to earthly marriage, it is clear within them that our earthly marriages stand as a mere shadow to our heavenly one. The scriptures begin,

"Husbands, love your wives, as Christ loved the church and gave himself up for her, that he might sanctify her, having cleansed her by the washing of water with the word, so that he might present the church to himself in splendor, without spot or wrinkle or any such thing, that she might be holy and without blemish. In the same way husbands should love their wives as their own bodies. He who loves his wife loves himself. For no one ever hated his own flesh, but nourishes and cherishes it, just as Christ does the church, because we are members of his body. "Therefore, a man shall leave his father and mother and hold fast to his wife, and the two shall become one flesh." This mystery is profound, and I am saying that it refers to Christ and the church. " As we truly reflect on these verses, we find that earthly marriage not only shadows our heavenly one but is also used by God to help refine and prepare us for our eternal marriage.

As a woman who grew up with many trust issues, I have found my own marriage to be extremely challenging. Yet, as I began to study and reflect more about how God really sees my earthly marriage, as a reflection of His marriage to me, it has helped me to realize the responsibility I've been entrusted with through the gift of marriage. I do not find it a coincidence that the Hebrew word for sanctify is the same one used for marriage. I find it beautiful that, not only does this mean my earthly marriage is used to refine me, but even for those who are not married, the same holds true, for everyone who belongs to Christ is already married to Christ. Therefore, each one of us is already participating in the sanctification process, already being cleansed by Him through the washing of water with the word. How we regard our earthly marriage reflects how we regard our heavenly one. I want to be sensitive here because I know not everyone is treated in the way that is pleasing to God in their earthly marriage, however I would like to present that, whatever your earthly marriage looks like, you can be pleasing to God as you live out your identity as Christ's bride.

To spend too much time here would require a whole other book, I won't say much more, but to emphasize the dignity of being part of an eternal marriage here and now as we belong to Christ, and our marriage to Christ is and should be primary as it is an eternal one. For those of us who are married, this awareness alone is enough to keep us rightly related to Christ even when it's difficult to stay rightly related to one another. One day we will stand before Him, and our spouse will not be there. He will present us to Himself, holy, spotless, and without blemish and in that moment, we will know that no matter how difficult or hard it has been here, He has faithfully loved us as He loves Himself. We will know that we have never once been a forsaken bride. Right now, is our time to live in the light of that moment, and to let Him wash us from anything that keeps us from realizing it.

CHAPTER 7

TWO BECOME ONE

The joyful parade reaches full crescendo as you approach the father's house where you will spend the next seven days in yada, getting to know your bridegroom most intimately in the bridal chamber, or *Huppah.* Your bridegroom has gone before you, and your heart leaps with the knowledge that he awaits you within the chamber where you will soon consummate the b'rit, your marriage covenant. Your heart beats wildly as you contemplate all that will take place in just a few moments. *"Let him kiss me with the kisses of his mouth! For your love is better than wine; your anointing oils are fragrant; your name is oil poured out; therefore, virgins love you. Draw me after you; let us run. The king has brought me into his chambers."* (Song of Solomon 1:2-4). These words dance around you, thrilling and terrifying you at the same time. Never more vulnerable, yet also never more eager to press into the wonder of this moment to discover both your bridegroom and yourself in ways that you never have before. You are thankful for the brief comfort you find in the familiarity your bridesmaids offer, as they help you out from the Aperion. Your best friend catches your eye, still behind the veil, and you take refuge in her smile as she blesses you one last time before you enter in, *"Eat, friend, drink and be drunk with love." (Song of Solomon 5:1b).* As you head into the covering of the Huppah, you know you will emerge a whole new creation, as one who has taken her place in God's creation of one where once two had been. *"Therefore, a man shall leave his father and mother and hold fast to his wife, and they shall become one flesh. And the man and his wife were both naked and were not ashamed."* (Genesis 2:24). *"Bone of my bones, flesh of my flesh; she shall be called Woman, because she was taken out of Man."* *(Genesis 2:23).* Your heart takes refuge in these sacred words as you step towards your bridegroom. Joy floods through every cell of your body as you bath in new awareness that God is just a present here as you and your bridegroom. His words and your fulfillment of them in this moment become like sacred blanket, covering you and inviting you back into the garden of His love and presence where you are free from any stain or shame that existed before the Fall. Like the very first couple He joined into marriage covenant, you are both free to be naked and unashamed in His presence. Here, you are most His as you become joined with the one He has chosen for you. You've entered His covering. Flesh tears, blood spills; the covenant is sealed, the two have become one.

UNDER THE HUPPAH IT IS DONE

Every other moment of the wedding builds up to this one, the moment the covenant is sealed and the two consummate physically what began spiritually. As the bride and bridegroom enter the Huppah to consummate the marriage, the friend of the bridegroom waits outside the door. Once the consummation has taken place, the sheet upon which the two sealed the consummation would be handed out for the friend of the bridegroom to display before a celebrating crowd. The sheet, often embroidered by the mother of the bride with the bride's initials, would be passed along to the bride's family for safekeeping as evidence that the family had secured a pure bride for the bridegroom. The sheet offered the bride evidence if her bridegroom should ever claim she was not a pure bride, and therefore seek to divorce her.

The blood upon the sheet was such an important aspect of the ancient Hebrew wedding that mothers of the bride would often tuck a small pouch of sheep's blood within the bride's dress to ensure that blood was present on the sheet. Once the blood was shown, the party on the outside could begin, as in essence the substance of the wedding had been fulfilled, what began spiritually by faith had now been realized in the flesh. Although there were still some aspects of the ceremony to still observe, the two had already become one, therefore the reason for the seven-day celebration was validated. While the party roared outside the Huppah, the bride and bridegroom had enough provisions tucked inside to continue enjoying their time getting to yada (know) one another. When the bride did finally emerge, she would be unveiled, for her covering had now become her husband. The Huppah, representing God's covering over His creation, created a sacred space for not only His prize creation of man and woman to take refuge in as they acknowledged their covenant with Him, but also to acknowledge God's creation of the covenant of marriage itself. For marriage was God's idea and creation. *"Then the LORD God said, 'It is not good that the man should be alone; I will make a helper fit for him.'"* (Genesis 2:18). Just as during the first marriage, God's presence covered His children as the two became one, so His presence was acknowledged as covering over His children during the ancient Hebrew wedding. Although, not visibly present, like a quiet overseer, His presence was acknowledged in every detail in the ancient Hebrew wedding.

There is one aspect of the ancient Hebrew wedding that, although was part of the ceremony, continued to be carried out throughout the remainder of the couple's life, in some way extending the sacred beauty found in God's creation of marriage long beyond the wedding day. *Mikvah* would continue in recognition of the Torah as a ritual act dividing two periods of time when marital relations were forbidden because the wife was in a state of Niddah, or menstruating. During this time, the wife and husband would stop marital relations until seven days after her last day of menstruation. After this, she would immerse herself in *Mikvah,* after which she and her husband would resume normal marital relations. As discussed in Chapter three, Mikvah was the name for a ritual pool of water used for ritual cleansing. As the wife fully immerged herself beneath the waters, she became ritually clean before God and pure, enabling her to present herself to her husband once again as a brand-new creation once more. In this way, the joy and fulfillment of remembering their place within God experienced on the wedding day was extending throughout the couple's life together as each month the bride was transformed through Mikvah and born again.

Although the custom of holding out the sheet died away many years ago, there are still remnants of the wedding custom of "cutting covenant of blood" often even today's modern weddings. For instance, the tradition of the bride and groom's family and guests being seated on separate sides of the aisle. The red carpet down the center of the aisle, signifies the blood covenant being sealed as both parties being joined in marriage and their families walk down the aisle, allowing two families to be joined into one. What about the fact that the man and his wife are joined at the altar? What happens at an alter? Something, or in this case, someone dies. At a wedding, the bride and groom both die to themselves to become one before God and men as witness. *"Therefore, a man shall leave his father and mother and hold fast to his wife, and the two shall become one flesh. So, they are no longer two, but one flesh." (Mark 10:7-8).*

Just as this portion of the ancient Hebrew wedding represented the culmination and fulfillment of the marriage covenant, so it was with us when Christ became one with His bride at the Cross. Naked and yet unashamed, He hung, making Himself completely vulnerable to His love for us. Flesh tore, blood and water spilled out, the open wounds caused by His scourging, leaving the veil of his flesh exposing his ribs, blood of His blood, flesh of His flesh, the two had become one.

"Then the man said, "This at last is bone of my bones   and flesh of my flesh; she shall be called Woman,   because she was taken out of Man." (Genesis 2:23)

We might rightfully ask ourselves how Jesus fulfilled these aspects of the wedding for us? First, how does the sheet with blood on it relate to our covenant being fulfilled in Christ? Well, before we can answer that, lets refer to Deuteronomy 22:13-19 where we can catch a glimpse for the purpose of the sheet from Old Testament scripture, *"If any man takes a wife and goes in to her and then hates her and accuses her of misconduct and brings a bad name upon her, saying, 'I took this woman, and when I came near her, I did not find in her evidence of virginity,' then the father of the young woman and her mother shall take and bring out the evidence of her virginity to the elders of the city in the gate. And the father of the young woman shall say to the elders, 'I gave my daughter to this man to marry, and he hates her; and behold, he has accused her of misconduct, saying, "I did not find in your daughter evidence of virginity." And yet this is the evidence of my daughter's virginity.' And they shall spread the cloak before the elders of the city. Then the elders of that city shall take the man and whip him, and they shall fine him a hundred shekels of silver and give them to the father of the young woman, because he has brought a bad name upon a virgin of Israel. And she shall be his wife. He may not divorce her all his days."* We find in this scripture that the sheet with blood on it represented a legal protection for a bride and her family against unjust claims of her impurity. Once the covenant and consummation took place, the blood upon the sheet pronounced the bride's new identity was sealed and could not be taken back, should even her husband want to. She had become one with God and her husband, and what had been done cannot be undone.

So, what is our legal representation as Christ's bride? To find this answer, we must refer to Jesus, who is not only our eternal Bridegroom, but also our High Priest, who alone can present us faultless before the Father. Romans 3:34-25 gives us a picture of where this blood comes from and what it accomplishes for us. *"Being justified freely by his grace through the redemption that is in Christ Jesus; Whom God has set forth to be a propitiation through faith in his blood, to declare his righteousness for the remission of sins that are past, through the forbearance of God."* To truly understand this verse, we must know what propitiation means. The short answer is that it means to satisfy. Because neither you nor I are a pure bride, we have no way to become one with Christ as His bride, So He paid the way for us through His own blood. When a young Hebrew man came to ask for the hand of a young Hebrew woman in covenant marriage, what he was in essence doing was asking to take full responsibility for her, and not just physically, but also spiritually as well. He would become fully responsible for her before God and others. Because of the hardness of sin, there are few men who truly took this to heart, therefore Jesus even said when asked about whether divorce was permitted, *"He said to them, 'Because of your hardness of heart Moses allowed you to divorce your wives, but from the beginning it was not so,'" (Matthew 19:8).* Jesus, being fully God and fully man, when coming to marry us, took full responsibility for His bride. That means because He became responsible for her spiritually as well as in every other way, He had to become the one to pay for her sin to present her spotless and wrinkle-free before the Father. Another definition for the word propitiation is "averting the wrath of God by offering a gift." This is what Jesus' death at the Cross accomplished for us, His bride. And just as the sheet upheld became a permanent, legally binding article that pointed back to moment in time when one sacrificed her purity to become one with another, so the Cross does the same for those of us who are Christ's bride. What God required of us, a pure, spotless, virgin bride for His Son, He provided through His Son.

This sacrifice brings great peace, rest, and joy to brides like me who struggle to believe that we've been made thoroughly clean. No matter how much I know, sometimes I still feel unclean. One of the hardest battles I have fought has been to let my trust in Christ's finished work become greater than my feelings about who I've been (and still struggle not to be.)

I've learned to let the words from Ephesians 5:29-32 offer my heart and mind a constant place to enter, and to experience who I truly became through Christ's sacrifice," *For no one ever hated his own flesh, but nourishes and cherishes it, just as Christ does the church, because we are members of his body. 'Therefore, a man shall leave his father and mother and hold fast to his wife, and the two shall become one flesh.' This mystery is profound, and I am saying that it refers to Christ and the church. "* Just like in earthly marriage, it's easy to see who truly has become one with their spouse based on how the two regard each other. There are heart-breaking situations where one spouse is more married to their partner than their partner is to them. However, we are blessed to know that Jesus fully regards us as His bride. There is never a time when He looks at our actions or attitude of heart and decides to withdraw His love and acceptance of us. Sadly, because many of us have been treated this way by others, it's easy to think God will do the same. This says more about our heart than His. His heart is constant towards us, and as we force ourselves to believe and trust His heart over our own, we will find ourselves displaying and radiating His beautiful heart to those around us, who perhaps without us, might never truly witness the distinction that exists between the way the world loves and the way God does.

We catch a prophetic picture of this truth in Revelation 19:13-14 where it says, *"He is clothed in a robe dipped in blood, and the name by which he is called is 'The Word of God'. And the armies of heaven, arrayed in fine linen, white and pure, were following him on white horses."* If you look closely, you might see yourself in this picture, as one of the armies of heaven, arrayed in fine linen, riding behind your Bridegroom, on a white horse, a symbol of Christ's victory over death and sin. Revelation 19:7-8 makes note of what we find ourselves arrayed in once again when it says, *"Let us rejoice and exult and give him the glory, for the marriage of the Lamb has come, and his Bride has made herself ready; it was granted her to clothe herself with the fine linen, bright and pure"-for the fine linen is the righteous deeds of the saints."* We will one day be dressed on the outside with what we are now adorning ourselves with on the inside, Christ's righteousness granted to us through His gift of grace. The blood upon His robe, which to us, appears as a symbol of His great victory over everything in the world that has separated Him from His bride, yet the world who has rejected Him, marks the symbol of this foretold wrath.

Just as the marriage supper of the Lamb represents a wedding feast for those who have chosen to enter God's grace, there will also be another feast going on down on earth for those who have refused. Revelation 19:17-21 paints a horrific picture of what will occur at that feast.

"Then I saw an angel standing in the sun, and with a loud voice he called to all the birds that fly directly overhead, "Come, gather for the great supper of God, to eat the flesh of kings, the flesh of captains, the flesh of mighty men, the flesh of horses and their riders, and the flesh of all men, both free and slave, both small and great." And I saw the beast and the kings of the earth with their armies gathered to make war against him who was sitting on the horse and against his army. And the beast was captured, and with it the false prophet who in its presence had done the signs by which he deceived those who had received the mark of the beast and those who worshiped its image. These two were thrown alive into the lake of fire that burns with sulfur. And the rest were slain by the sword that came from the mouth of him who was sitting on the horse, and all the birds were gorged with their flesh."

As I contemplate these two contrasting feasts that we will one day literally step into through the fulfillment of God's prophetic word, I can't help but imagine how we, in some ways are already stepping into them through our earthly journeys right now as we feast upon Christ, our living Bread, and participate in communion with Him, entering fellowship with Him. In contrast, those outside of this communion feast upon false idols. They gorge upon this world. So that, when these events take place, they will only be an extension of how we've already been living our whole lives in Him. The coming moments in history will represents the culmination in the journey we've been headed towards our whole lives as Christ's bride, or as one married to this dying world.

And just like the ancient Hebrew bride, we will appear unveiled, for our covering will have surely taken place within our Bridegroom's presence. Like a bride bursting forth from the Huppah after her consummation has taken place, with joyous wonder, we will burst from our heavenly Huppah to enter back into the earths domain to ride forth in His victory, a victory that has also become ours through His redeeming grace.

As we consider the veil and how the bride would be unveiled by her husband once his covering as taken place, we must ask ourselves, how does Christ remove our veil?

To consider this, we must go back to the Cross and consider what happened there. John 19:30-37 point us to the moment when our consummation was made complete.

"When Jesus had received the sour wine, he said, 'It is finished,' and he bowed his head and gave up his spirit. Since it was the day of

Preparation, and so that the bodies would not remain on the cross on the Sabbath (for that Sabbath was a high day), the Jews asked Pilate that their legs might be broken and that they might be taken away. So, the soldiers came and broke the legs of the first, and of the other who had been crucified with him. But when they came to Jesus and saw that he was already dead, they did not break his legs. But one of the soldiers pierced his side with a spear, and at once there came out blood and water. He who saw it has borne witness—his testimony is true, and he knows that he is telling the truth—that you also may believe. For these things took place that the Scripture might be fulfilled: 'Not one of his bones will be broken.' And again another Scripture says, 'They will look on him whom they have pierced.'"

Mark 15:33-38 gives us a glimpse of the exact moment that our veil was removed, forever inviting us into oneness with God and fellowship with our Father.

"And when the sixth hour had come, there was darkness over the whole land until the ninth hour. And at the ninth hour Jesus cried with a loud voice, "Eloi, Eloi, lema sabachthani?" which means, "My God, my God, why have you forsaken me?" And some of the bystanders hearing it said, "Behold, he is calling Elijah." And someone ran and filled a sponge with sour wine, put it on a reed and gave it to him to drink, saying, "Wait, let us see whether Elijah will come to take him down." And Jesus uttered a loud cry and breathed his last. And the curtain of the temple was torn in two, from top to bottom."

"My God, why have you forsaken me?" Even if we haven't had the courage to ask it out loud, we've all thought it at one point in our lives. Yet only Jesus has truly ever experienced what it feels like to have God turn His back on you completely. While the darkness of the whole world pressed fully against the head and heart of our heavenly Bridegroom, absorbing into Him all the poison that's ever kept us away from Him, God waited for the moment the consummation was complete, the moment Christ's blood fully covered over each one of our hearts. And at last, the moment came: *"It is finished!"* And at that, the veil was torn, as for the first time since Adam and Eve were cast out of the garden, and away from God's presence, every man, woman, and child, was invited back in.

Jesus' work was complete, He at last rested from all His work in securing a forever safe place for His bride to enter His rest.

"Thus, the heavens and the earth were finished, and all the host of them. And on the seventh day God finished his work that he had done, and he rested on the seventh day from all his work that he had done. So God blessed the seventh day and made it holy, because on it God rested from all his work that he had done in creation." (Genesis 2:1-3).

Hebrews 10: 19-23 , " *Therefore, brothers, since we have confidence to enter the holy places by the blood of Jesus, by the new and living way that he opened for us through the curtain, that is, through his flesh, and since we have a great priest over the house of*

God, let us draw near with a true heart in full assurance of faith, with our hearts sprinkled clean from an evil conscience and our bodies washed with pure water. Let us hold fast the confession of our hope without wavering, for he who promised is faithful."

Veil lifted, eyes clear, we behold our beloved Bridegroom, and within Him, ourselves as a new creation, who we've always been in Him, yet never allowed ourselves to be because of sin's ever looming darkness within and all around. As Paul says in 2 Corinthians 3:18, *"And we all, with unveiled face, beholding the glory of the Lord, are being transformed into the same image from one degree of glory to another. For this come from the Lord who is Spirit."*

As I contemplate how to end this portion of our time together, I am reminded of the first time I saw myself as Christ's bride, with unveiled face. It still wrecks me that He does this for us, allows us the opportunity, even while still clad in clumsy, earthbound feet, to see ourselves in Him, a glimpse that can only be described as supernatural. I was cleaning out a cabinet in my kitchen when I discovered a box I had stowed away after our wedding. As I pulled the box out, it spilled several copies of our wedding program all over the floor. I had not seen the program in years, therefore had forgotten all about the poem we had published on the front cover, one I had written for my husband a few months before our wedding day. As I poured over the once familiar words, I came to the sudden realization that although they were meant for my earthly husband, they were being received right then as words to my heavenly one. Tears flooded my eyes as I began to feel myself as Christ's heavenly bride. As a woman who spent so many years bathed in the darkest parts this world has to offer, it is truly a wondrous miracle to experience a heart within you that has been, *"cleansed…by the washing of water with the word…holy, and without blemish."* (see Ephesians 5:26-27). With that, I would like to close this chapter by inviting you into that experience. As you read the words below, I pray that you too, might enter what it is to be Christ's bride, to know that His hands have been washing you, that He's tenderly cared for you as His own body because you are His beloved Bride.

"I in them and you in me, that they may become perfectly one, so that the world may know that you sent me and loved them even as you loved me." - Jesus (John 17:23)

Like a river runs, forever to the sea

Our love is tracing a path to eternity

An endless journey, you and I choose to trace

This precious gift of love, granted in God's most precious grace

So underserving, so unworthy, so scared by sin

God burst through the door to let His light shine in

You are the light that has come to shine on my face

Capturing my heart, taking me to unknown places

I catch my breath, I still can't conceive

God granted a miracle that I still can't believe

I dreamt of you, I hoped for so long

My heart became hardened, but it's now the joy of my song

I forgot about the dream, the echoes of my past

And prayed for God to give me a love that would last

It was my Father in heaven who then took my hand

And gently helped me submit to the power of His plan

How unworthy we are to the miracle of love

A gift of such sacrifice can only come from above

I was once was a lonely sinner, but now I am complete

His grace makes me whole as I worship at His feet

Now O am ready to lay hold of God's plan

As I reach out to you and take hold of your hand

I see the miracle of you unfolding in place

Each time my hand touches your face

I look at you and I can't help but see

The man God created just for me

I am blessed beyond measure, My heart overflows

With unbinding love, more precious as it grows

Of all God's creation, I'm certain very few

Match the beauty and love I find in the miracle of you.

Chapter 8

Seven Days Inside, Seven Circles Abide

"Leah," your name whispered through his lips sound like the song you've waited your whole life to hear. Never more vulnerable and yet safe at the same time. Feelings and emotions you've never experienced pulse through your body, soul, and spirit, making you feel more alive than you ever felt. *"Bone of my bone, flesh of my flesh..."* (Genesis 3:23), perhaps these words explain how you feel as if you've finally landed exactly where you've always belonged, at his side, near his heart.

The sounds of celebration bounce and sway around you, almost like an exclamation mark resounding over the joy you feel within, inviting you and your beloved to experience the expanse of this wedding bliss into joy of those celebrating. You sense the impending moment when this experience will be over, when you will emerge to circle your beloved bridegroom seven times as the seven blessings of creation are read over you, your part in extending evidence of God's creation, your chance to enter in to His great story of wonder as you testify to His words still here, breaking through His creation, bearing witness to the power of His sovereignty, even over the darkest of times. *"Hear , O Israel: The LORD our God, the LORD is one. You shall love the LORD your God with all your heart and with all your soul and with all your might."* (Deuteronomy 6:4-9). He's still here, still carrying us as we carry through His divine plan here on earth. Even this moment bears witness to His faithfulness towards us, *"Israel, for you have striven with God and with men, and have prevailed."* (Genesis 32:28). One day, God will allow my body to carry forth more of His children through this covenant that we are fulfilling right now and the promise that He first gave to our father Abraham will burst forth through me. *"I will establish my covenant between me and you and your offspring after you throughout their generations for an everlasting covenant, to be God to you and your offspring after you."* (Genesis 17:7). Two become One, allowing the opportunity to expand God's oneness through us through childbirth. *Oh, the depth of the riches and wisdom and knowledge of God! How unsearchable are His judgements and how inscrutable his ways!"* (Romans 11:33). He carries us as we carry His image throughout our lives, leaving unmistakable evidence here upon earth's dusty surface that, surely God has been here.

The Encircling

For seven days, the bride and bridegroom are in the Huppah, emerging briefly to interact and celebrate with their guests, yet ever returning to reacquaint themselves with one another. On the last day, they will emerge to have one last ritual observed before the celebration will culminate in the Wedding Feast. This last ritual will involve the bride walking around her groom seven times. Seven is the number for completion in the Bible. God created the world in six days, and rested on the seventh, therefore leaving even rest as an extension of His joy felt for His creation. As the unveiled bride encircles her bridegroom, she is not pointing to what will be, but is publicly proclaiming what already is. Her covering from both her husband and God has been made complete. She's now a completed bride, perfectly aligned with her Creator and her circling her beloved is an expression of that alignment. God has encircled them, and not just them, but everyone who belongs to Him and is willing to acknowledge His rightful place in their hearts and history, as well as their rightful response to Him, which is to revolve around Him, and not He around us. The number seven is woven through-out scripture and stands as a seal for God's perfect and complete creation.

Here are few examples from scripture that refers to how God uses the number seven as a signature of His perfect and complete work: In the creation story,

"Thus, the heavens and the earth were finished, and all the host of them. And on the seventh day God finished his work that he had done, and he rested on the seventh day from all his work that he had done. So, God blessed the seventh day and made it holy, because on it God rested from all his work that he had done in creation." (Genesis 2:1-3)

In God's prescribed sacrificial system,

"You shall do the same with your oxen and with your sheep: seven days it shall be with its mother; on the eighth day you shall give it to me." (Exodus 22:30)

In the healing of Naaman from leprosy,

"And Elisha sent a messenger to him, saying, "Go and wash in the Jordan seven times, and your flesh shall be restored, and you shall be clean." (2 Kings 5:10)

In the fall of Jericho,

"You shall march around the city, all the men of war going around the city once. Thus, shall you do for six days. Seven priests shall bear seven trumpets of rams' horns before the ark. On the seventh day you shall march around the city seven times, and the priests shall blow the trumpets." (Joshua 6:3-4)

In the lamps to light the menorah in the tabernacle,

"You shall make seven lamps for it. And the lamps shall be set up so as to give light on the space in front of it." (Exodus 25:37)

These are just few examples of how God uses the number seven in the Bible to demonstrate His perfect completion over all He does and creates. We can contrast it with the number six, which is used to symbolize man. Man was made on the sixth day of creation, and we know that in Bible prophesy, the number six has direct correlation to the enemy. We find reference to this in Revelation 13:18 which says, *"These calls for wisdom: let the one who has understanding calculate the number of the beast, for it is the number of a man, and his number is 666."* No matter how many times you repeat six, it will never become seven. Just as we, mere men, no matter how much we strive for completion, will always fall short. Just as Romans 3:23 points out, *"for all have sinned and fall short of the glory of God."* Even Christ's death on the cross alludes to His dying for the sin of man as the darkness of God's wrath upon Him began at the sixth hour as shown in Luke 23:44, *"It was now about the sixth hour, and there was darkness over the whole land until the ninth hour."* Yet, just as in the creation story, God rested from all His works on the seventh day, so we find Jesus rested from His on the Sabbath, the seventh day of the week. Hebrews assures us that this rest from works is still available for those of us who belong to Christ. In fact, to not enter the rest and completion of all Christ did for us upon the Cross is considered disobedience as expressed in Hebrews 4:9-10, *"So then, there remains a Sabbath rest for the people of God, for whoever has entered God's rest has also rested from his works as God did from his."*

Just as the Hebrew bride walked seven circles around her groom to display who she had become through his covering, so we, Christ's bride, walk through this world in His rest, a display of His perfect completion over us. Because we are His, we have left the six of man, which will always fall short, and entered the seven of God, which renders us complete through Christ's finished work to cover our sin and render us whole before our Father in heaven. Perhaps, Revelation 1:4 best displays the role that seven plays as we, the bride of Christ encircle Him as it says, *"John to the seven churches that are in Asia: Grace to you and peace from him who is and who was and who is to come, and from the seven spirits who are before his throne"* The letters to the churches which are mentioned during the first three chapters in Revelation, represent not only the churches present at the time John wrote the letters from Christ through His Revelation to His bride, but they also represent Christ's words to her throughout the church age. The seven spirits who are referred to in these scriptures and the subsequent ones, thereafter, represent Christ's Holy Spirit, alive and active within His bride, the church. The amazing thing about these letters is not just the fact that they allude to the number seven, again, bearing witness to Christ's completion and oneness with them through the power of the Holy Spirit, but also how, in God's sovereignty, the actual physical locations that these churches existed at the time literally created a circle, a church circuit from which each letter would pass through to be read by and through each church, before being dispersed to the other churches that existed within the other cities of Roman Asia. Although other churches existed during this time, Christ chose to use these seven churches as an expression of His completeness within the whole church body. The seven spirits, seven eyes (Revelation5:6), and seven-torches of fire (Revelation 4:5) express His perfect and complete omnipresence, and omniscience.

The seven days spent within the Huppah during an ancient Hebrew wedding were called The Week of the Bride. Isaiah 26:20-21 alludes to the week of the bride when it says, *"Come, my people, enter your chambers, and shut your doors behind you; hide yourselves for a little while until the fury has passed by.*

For behold, the Lord is coming out from his place   to punish the inhabitants of the earth for their iniquity, and the earth will disclose the blood shed on it,   and will no more cover its slain."

Daniel 9:27 also speaks about this week, the seven-day period when, while the bride is tucked safely away in the chamber with her Bridegroom, the world, at that time under the authority of the antichrist, will be going through an altogether different sort of consummation with God's Word. *"And he shall make a strong covenant with many for one week, and for half of the week he shall put an end to sacrifice and offering. And on the wing of abominations shall come one who makes desolate, until the decreed end is poured out on the desolator."*

There is a time coming soon when Christ will have His bride as she experiences the fullness and completeness of all she's become through Him. While she is entering into the culmination of all she's become through her completeness in Christ, the world will be experiencing what it means to be outside Christ. Daniel 12:1-4 assures us, *"At that time shall arise Michael, the great prince who has charge of your people. And there shall be a time of trouble, such as never has been since there was a nation till that time. But at that time your people shall be delivered, everyone whose name shall be found written in the book. And many of those who sleep in the dust of the earth shall awake, some to everlasting life, and some to shame and everlasting contempt. And those who are wise shall shine like the brightness of the sky above; and those who turn many to righteousness, like the stars forever and ever. But you, Daniel, shut up the words and seal the book, until the time of the end. Many shall run to and fro, and knowledge shall increase."* While we, Christ's bride, will be experiencing the consolation of our faith in Christ, those left in the world will be given one last chance to enter Christ's atonement, only this time the invitation comes through suffering. During this time, all eyes will be turned towards Israel, God's original chosen land and people. What He began will be fulfilled, even as the antichrist tries his best to stop it.

The seven lamps, seven seals, seven torches of fire, seven stars, seven days in a week, seven years of tribulation, and seven days with his bride all point to God's perfect completion over His creation, yet there is one place in scripture where the number takes on new depth. In Revelation 5, we are invited to gaze upon Jesus, our Bridegroom, as the culmination of all He is to us comes into full view. It begins, *"Then I saw in the right hand of him who was seated on the throne a scroll written within and on the back, sealed with seven seals. And I saw a mighty angel proclaiming with a loud voice, "Who is worthy to open the scroll and break its seals?" And no one in heaven or on earth or under the earth was able to open the scroll or to look into it, and I began to weep loudly because no one was found worthy to open the scroll or to look into it. And one of the elders said to me, "Weep no more; behold, the Lion of the tribe of Judah, the Root of David, has conquered, so that he can open the scroll and its seven seals." And between the throne and the four living creatures and among the elders I saw a Lamb standing, as though it had been slain, with seven horns and with seven eyes, which are the seven spirits of God sent out into all the earth. And he went and took the scroll from the right hand of him who was seated on the throne. And when he had taken the scroll, the four living creatures and the twenty-four elders fell down before the Lamb, each holding a harp, and golden bowls full of incense, which are the prayers of the saints."* The seven seals within this scroll represent the beginning of God's wrath being poured upon the world. Considering this, we might wonder why John wept so strongly that these seals could not be opened. Tucked within these scriptures that point to the judgment coming upon the world, we catch an even more profound glimpse of our beloved Bridegroom, the Lamb, standing as though it had been slain. Notice the seven horns on His head, representing His perfect and complete power, the seven eyes, which represent the seven spirits of God (alluded to also in 1:4). John is weeping because no one was found worthy to open the scrolls or to look into them. He senses the tension that exists for the church, whose very existence depends upon God's fulfillment of His Word being carried forth. Unless there is an intercessor that could allow heaven and earth to be reconciled and brought back into God's covering, the church could not be saved. Therefore, our Bridegroom makes His appearance in the one form that both connects us back to Him and displays His victory over all that ever divided us form Him," *And they sang a new song, saying, "Worthy are you to take the scroll   and to open its seals, for you were slain, and by your blood you ransomed people for God from every tribe and language and people and nation, and you have made them a kingdom and priests to our God, and they shall reign on the earth."* (Revelation 5:9-10).

Your Bridegroom, beloved, is the Lamb of God. *"All we like sheep have gone astray; we have turned—every one—to his own way; and the Lord has laid on him the iniquity of us all." (Isaiah 53:6).*

Each one of us will enter eternity with our Bridegroom because He came for us as a lamb, bearing our ever-wandering identity upon Himself so we might have the chance to become who He alone knew we were always meant to be, His beloved bride.

There are times I wander, and those times will often lead me to wonder if I really am His. Yet, each time, He comes for me as the Lamb, and as I gaze upon Him, I am reminded that my oneness in Him has never been and will never be based upon who I am or what I have done (or not done), but solely upon who He is. And because He chose to love me and sacrifice Himself for me, all I can do is ever say, "yes, I will belong to You." The miracle of His grace is experienced each time I exit me and enter back into who He's caused me to become as the Lamb of God, slain for everything that could ever divide me from Him.

This truth is expressed perfectly in that the word Kalah (Bride) and Chatan (groom) do not even exist in the Bible to refer to a bride and groom, but only to define a daughter –in –law or son-in-law. For God did not see the need for such words as they were never intended to be separate. In defining one, you separate them from one another. Therefore, when we see the Lamb of God appearing as the slain, we see Him as one with us. And ten thousand years from now, when you and I are both in our glorified bodies, Jesus will still bear the marks of His purchase for us upon His skin, an eternal reminder of His sacrifice to make us one forever in Him.

Therefore, beloved bride, I pray that when you are tempted to see yourself apart from Him, you might remember the Lamb who bears the marks of His oneness with you and be reminded of the truth of who you've become in Him, and return.

"...Come, I will show you the bride, the wife of the Lamb." And he carried me away in the Spirit to a great, high mountain, and showed me the holy city Jerusalem coming down out of heaven from God, having the glory of God, its radiance like a most rare jewel, like a jasper, clear as crystal." (Revelation 21:9-11)

"And I saw no temple in the city, for its temple is the Lord God Almighty and the Lamb. And the city has no need of sun or moon to shine on it, for the glory of God gives it light, and its lamp is the Lamb." (Revelation 21:22-23)

Not long ago I was at a retreat where I dared to ask Jesus to show me the truth about how He sees me. At once, in my heart I could see a beautiful banquet table that stretched as far as the eye could see, and I knew He was seated at the end, waiting to dine with whoever was willing to come. And I saw myself, dressed beautifully, beckoning others to come and dine with Him at the table, and rushing over to excitedly seat everyone who agreed to take their place at the table.

I knew this was true about me, yet I could sense that He wanted me to ask Him the truth about how He wants to see me. My heart filled with conviction as I at once saw myself seated right beside Him, leaning in to such intimacy that I could scarcely stand it. As our eyes met, I was seen, cherished, and loved. It is terrifying and yet wonderful to become this exposed and vulnerable to Love, yet I knew this is what I was made for yet had often been so fearful to enter into for myself. This time, I was not running around and inviting others to the table, but instead had one outstretched hand held out beside me, like an open invitation to anyone willing to enter into this unbroken fellowship with Love, Himself, our Bridegroom, Jesus.

So, as we close, I invite you to the table.

And I leave you with the words that He spoke over my heart as I took my place at the table and asked Him, "LORD, is this the end of me?" and He responded, "No, it's only the beginning"

And I saw the holy city, new Jerusalem, coming down out of heaven from God, prepared as a bride adorned for her husband. And I heard a loud voice from the throne saying, "Behold, the dwelling place of God is with man. He will dwell with them, and they will be his people and God himself will be with them as their God." (Revelation 21:3)